The
Pearl
PERSPECTIVE

Copyright

Copyright © 2018 by Jennifer Webb

All rights reserved. This printed book, ebook or any portion thereof may not be reproduced or used in any manner whatsoever without the express written permission of the publisher.

contentmentquesting.com |
jennifer@contentmentquesting.com

Disclosure

This book contains affiliate links. If you click on a link and make a purchase, then I will receive a small commission at no extra cost to you. Thank you for your support! For more information, please see the disclosure on my blog.

Dedication

To Shanon, who has always believed in me, encouraged me, and been the wind beneath my wings.

To my sweet sons, who continually light up my life.

To all my readers because who wants to write a book without people to read it?

The Pearl Perspective:

How Changing Your Perspective Can Change Your Life

By: Jennifer Webb

contentmentquesting.com

Table of Contents

Copyright --- 2

Disclosure --- 3

Dedication: --- 4

Table of Contents -- 5

Acknowledgement -- 7

Foreword: -- 8

Chapter 1: -- 1
    The Pearl -- *1*

Chapter 2: -- 8
    Change Your Perspective: The Power of Positivity ----------------------- *8*

Chapter 3: -- 12
    Mindfulness -- *12*

Chapter 4: -- 17
    Letting Go of Worry --- *17*

Chapter 5: --- 26
   Why Comparing Yourself to Others Is a Trap -------------------------------- *26*

Chapter 6: --- 33
   Self-Care -- *33*

Chapter 7: --- 41
   The Power of Gratitude -- *41*

Chapter 8: --- 49
   Self-Talk --- *49*

Chapter 9: --- 58
   Dealing with the Past and Pushing Through Hard Times ------------------ *58*

Chapter 10: -- 70
   Setting Goals and Chasing Your Dreams ------------------------------------- *70*

Chapter 11: -- 83
   Choices --- *83*

Chapter 12: -- 90
   Handling Critics and Criticism --- *90*

Chapter 13: -- 97
   Building Your Support Network --- *97*

Chapter 14: --- 105
   Wrapping It All Up --- *105*

About The Author: -- 108

Acknowledgement

Special thanks to:

My Editor: Amber Knoles.

Amber, you have been an amazing guide and support through this whole process. You have been uplifting and encouraging to me, not to mention having endless patience with all the revisions. This book would not be what it is without you.

My friends, book launch team, beta readers, and fellow bloggers including, but not limited to:

Nikki Warren

Amy Coleman

Anna Ledonne

Christine Walker

Sharon Easterling

Gail Vaden

Suzi Whitford

Tami Walker

Nadalie Bardowell

Heather LeGuilloux

Lucy Smith

Jennifer Winsor

My family and other friends that continue to support me in all my endeavors. Thank you.

Foreword:

Hello friend. I'm so glad you are here. Life is too short to simply spend going through the motions. If you are ready to start enjoying your life more, and taking steps to change it, you picked the right book. Consider this a personal letter from me to you, or like we are sitting down beside one another having a friendly chat.

I want you to know up-front that I believe in God. I could not write an inspirational book without mentioning HIM. I don't intend for it to be preachy, but I do intend to show you my heart and the tremendous amount of myself that I have put into this book. I believe in a personal loving God that uses our trials as lessons to show us how to grow as people. He's real, he's loving, and he's with me every single day, no matter what I am going through. My trust and faith in him is absolute, but far from perfect. I also want you to know that whatever you may be going through, I am praying for you.

I want to share with you the things that I have learned throughout my life about the things that make it better. What works, and what doesn't work. Some things and mindsets we need to cling to, others we must let go. It's much like cleaning your house. Some things clutter up your life, while others add value and enjoyment.

While you may not feel like a pearl right now, I want to use this book to show you that you are. You are beautiful, valuable, and unique. You have something to offer the world that no one else has. No one else has your unique perspective on life, your unique experiences, or your thoughts.

I can't wait to see you shine!

Praise For "The Pearl Perspective"

"This book is incredible, I got hooked and couldn't put it down. I have read many self-development books and this is one of my favorites. It is full of simple action steps that you can add into your life straight away to start seeing improvements. If you are looking to improve your mindset and life I highly recommend this book."

Lucy Smith, Personal Development coach and Blogger at <u>Succeed Now</u>

"This book is wonderful! Jennifer gives practical and useful advice that can help you change both your perspective and your life. And it's written in a way that holds your attention, like a friend is talking to you over coffee."

-Tami Walker, blogger, <u>The Inspiration Lady</u>

"I read a few chapters, it's wonderful! Thank you for being brave and sharing your advice with the world!"

Suzi Whitford, <u>Start A Mom Blog</u>

"Lots of good information! The author included tidbits of real life experience that made for an entertaining and highly enjoyable read. Highly recommend!"

–Nikki W. Mom and Business Owner

"I've officially finished reading your book, and I enjoyed it immensely. The writing style is casual and easy to read, yet still knowledgeable and inspiring. The content itself is solid, and I love that you backed it up with credible sources. I still felt like I could relate to a lot of what you said."

Anna Ledonne, Psychology Major

Chapter 1:

The Pearl

When I was twenty-one, I worked a summer job as a lab assistant in a microbiology lab at a local community college. It paid minimum wage, but it was interesting work that I enjoyed, with a flexible schedule that allowed me to take some summer classes. It was the perfect summer job for me. Over the two summers I worked there, the chemistry professor, Dr. Battles, became my mentor, and we struck up a friendship.

It was a good experience overall, but one lesson stuck with me, and still inspires me to this day.

An Unconventional Lesson

I saw a visitor enter the lab, and I looked up from my work. I smiled when I saw that it was Dr. Battles. The cold, fluorescent lighting illuminated hard surfaces, test tubes, and an ancient autoclave in the corner next to the sink. The bacteria incubator was in the back, along with shelves of microscopes. Some might have found it an odd work environment, but I felt right at home in a classroom lab setting.

Since I usually visited Dr. Battles in his office, I wondered about the purpose of his visit. Was he here to ask me "Does a possum have lips?" as he was fond of doing? (I still don't know the answer, and why he always chose that particular question as a conversation opener is still a mystery.) He was brilliant despite his silliness, and his life lessons usually came in an unconventional manner.

He was carrying a wooden box. Without a word, he came to stand in front of me and opened it. Inside were a handful of white marbles and a single black one.

"Did you come to show me that you finally found all your marbles?" I cracked. "Or are you still looking for some of them?"

"Ha, ha," he replied, clearly not amused by my witty remark. He drew his bushy eyebrows together, fastened his gaze on me, and asked, "What do you see?"

I knew him well enough to guess that he was about to deliver one of his cryptic life lessons. "Marbles." I replied.

"Look closer," he said.

I tried, but I still saw marbles rolling around inside a wooden box. Why were they in a box? Most people kept them in a bag that got shoved in desk drawer and forgotten. "I see marbles rolling around in a wooden box," I said.

"Nope." He probed me further. "Think about what they could be. What do you see?"

"Pearls?" I guessed. I could imagine them as pearls.

He must have been pleased by the remark, because he smiled and said, "Right." Then he continued, "Jennifer, when you walk into that classroom next fall, remember what you see in this box. These are your students. Most people will see them as plain marbles, but if you look closely, you'll see what they really are: they're pearls. **Each of us is a pearl. We are all special and precious in the sight of the Lord. It is up to you to see your students like that, and to teach them their true worth."**

Now that wooden box of marbles made sense. I looked at it with a new perspective. Then I tried to imagine what it would be like when I graduated next year and got a real job teaching. I envisioned myself standing in front of a room of students, a pearl hidden in each one of them, waiting to be discovered.

The change in my perspective must have shown on my face, because when I looked back up at Dr. Battles, he had a broad smile on his face.

Then he told me, "Take one of the marbles, and keep it to remind you of what I just told you."

I looked at the box of "pearls" and considered which one to choose. The white ones were pretty, but the one that really called to me was the single black one. Not only had it become a pearl in my eyes, but it was also different from the rest, unique. That meant it was the most valuable of the bunch.

I took the marble and asked him, "Are they really pearls?" and he scoffed.

"What do you think?" he said with a laugh, and turned to exit the room.

His story stuck with me. I hope it sticks with you too.

Sharing My Pearl Perspective

Four years later, after what felt like a short lifetime, I stood onstage at the school awards ceremony in May of 2007. Hundreds of eyes were on me. As I looked out past the lights to the teenage crowd, I knew this was the last time that I would ever see these precious "kids" assembled like this, and I wanted to say something to them that would make an impact. I wanted to tell them how special they were, how much I loved them, and how much of an impact they had on me.

I can't remember my exact words, but I remember speaking from my heart. I related the story of Dr. Battles and the pearls. I said that I loved them, and it had been my privilege to teach them for the past three years. I made sure they knew that I believed in each of them and thought they were special, that they were my pearls—special, precious, and unique. I could not see very well because of the lights shining in my face. I knew my principal and some of the higher administrators were watching, but I didn't care. This was my chance. I needed to say these things to my kids before I left them. I finished my story and gave my awards, then turned to walk offstage for the last time.

Much to my surprise, I saw the sweet veteran history teacher stand as he clapped. I was confused. I thought he'd already given his awards? Then, in a wave, I saw people standing and clapping throughout the auditorium. I thought my heart was about to explode out of my chest—in a good way. Tears sprang to my eyes and I felt the back of my throat close up. I put my hand over my mouth. The administrators that I thought were about to pull me off the stage were standing with tears in their eyes and clapping!

In that moment, I realized what an impact my words must have had on them. I felt love and satisfaction wrap around me in a giant bear hug and I knew that these past three years had not been wasted. All the struggles, all the time and emotion that I had poured into my work, was worth it. Teaching, for me, was not just a job, but a huge part of my life. Each of these kids had a little piece of my heart, and as I told them, I genuinely cared about each of them. People can tell if you are faking it when it comes to caring.

I had always said that if the Lord was able to use me to make a difference to just one person that the struggles of my teaching journey would be worth it. This moment, I felt, was the answer to that prayer.

Hope in the Midst of Struggling

Have you ever felt like you have been called to do something, but once you get in there and start doing it, you struggle? I always felt like I was doing the right thing when teaching, but it was HARD—harder than I ever dreamed possible. There were days during the first year that I prayed, "Lord, please help me get through this day. Help me make it through one more day." Then, there were other days that I prayed "Oh dear Lord, PLEASE help me make it through fifth period!"

Fifth period was the longest class, the biggest class, and it was also right before lunch, when I taught my most challenging students. No matter how hard I tried to keep our lessons on track, they talked back. They were experts at asking off-topic questions. Labs were unpredictable at best, and disastrous at worst. One in particular stands out: I completely lost control of the class and our lab, which was supposed to be about infectious diseases and how they spread, became, "how do we most effectively spread baby powder all over the classroom?" In my eyes, I was the only one to blame. I stood there wondering how much powder could collect around the desks before we all started making snowmen. At the end of the day, my colleague found me sweeping up the mess, and when she asked, "What happened in here?" I burst into tears.

There were days that I doubted, days that I wondered what in the world I thought I was doing standing up in front of that class, trying to keep order and teach. I was exhausted emotionally, physically, and mentally. I was overwhelmed. I worked harder than I had ever worked in my entire life, yet it still did not seem to be enough. I could not connect with those kids! Sometimes on my lunch breaks, on especially bad days, I would turn out the lights, lock my door, and hide in a corner to cry while I ate my lunch. Here I was, the supposed teacher, and I felt like I was the one who needed to be sitting in one of the desks.

On those days, I would come home and look at the black marble that Dr. Battles had given me, and that's all I saw: a black marble. I saw something worthless, something that stood out like a sore thumb in a box of white marbles. It didn't even shine.

Have you ever looked at your life like that? Have you ever felt like your life has become a trap instead of something to be enjoyed, like a dull, worthless black marble that sticks out like a sore thumb, in contrast to what you wished it looked like?

I had signed a nine-month contract, and I needed the job because we had to eat and keep a roof over our heads. It seemed like I made every mistake I could possibly make during those first nine months. Yet, I looked down the hall and saw a veteran teacher that actually seemed to ENJOY and THRIVE. How did she do that?! What kind of pixie dust did she have hidden in her desk?

She connected with her students, and she loved the literature that she taught them. Discipline came easy to her, the classroom ran smoothly, and there was a lot of learning taking place. More than that... the kids loved her! What?! How did she achieve that when I felt like I was gearing up for war every day?

I was too exhausted to explore the answer. I got up at 5 am and worked until 9 pm every day, grading papers and planning my next day's lessons. I took home more homework than my students did, except I actually DID mine. Still, I kept trudging, going through the motions. I was trying imperfectly, but I was still trying. I was not ready to give up.

Have you ever felt broken, ready to give up, but something inside you just wouldn't allow it? Has there ever been a time in your life when you felt like you were barely making it and you said to yourself, "There has GOT to be another way!"?

Chapter 2:

Change Your Perspective: The Power of Positivity

My attitude, which had started off as, "I can do anything! I am here to change the world, one person at a time!" slowly started to go south. Exhaustion took its toll on me, and day after day, month after month, my dream was slowly dying. I was giving it my all, and my all was not enough.

As the days slowly counted down, my attitude slipped into one that I despised – the "I don't care" and "whatever" attitude. We do this to shield ourselves. What you don't care about can't hurt you, right? The problem is that it's not true. When you decide not to care, that decision hurts others in addition to yourself. The ironic thing about a bad attitude is that sometimes you don't realize the harm it's causing. I certainly didn't.

I told myself that I didn't care. My attitude became just as negative as others in the teacher's lounge, because at the time it felt good to privately let off a bit of steam. What I didn't realize was that venting my frustrations sabotaged both myself and my students. My attitude came out in my teaching. My lectures could have put a hyperactive energizer bunny to sleep. They were flat. I felt flat-- and trapped.

"I don't care" is far easier to say than it is to actually live.

A New Start

Things slowly started to get better. By the end of the school year, I decided I would do better the next year, and hoped my first year of teaching wasn't as much of a disaster as I feared.

Over the summer, we attended mandatory in-service training. I was excited about it because some of my other teacher friends would be there, and surely there was some secret that I could learn to make the upcoming year go better. I was determined not to let my second year be a train wreck.

Most of the training was pretty dull, but one made an impact. The instructor shared a story about his first year of teaching that mirrored my own. I nearly cried, because it struck such a chord with me. My own heart broke as he described getting hit in the head with a bunch of paper wads as he was trying to teach, and starting to cry because he felt like his dream was dying. I very much knew how he must have felt.

Then, he went on to talk about love languages and concrete strategies that I could use in my room, like time management and classroom management. I tried to soak it up like a sponge and took tons of notes. He also talked about attitudes, and because of his talk, I realized that mine had become the attitude that I least wanted to have. He talked about the power of cultivating a more positive outlook, but most of all, he talked about loving the students.

I learned that caring is not a bad thing. Caring makes a huge difference.

The Secret Was Out

I don't remember that speaker's name, but I still remember how he made me feel. That is one of the major ways we impact others: **they might not remember our names, but will always remember how we made them feel**. After the year I had, I felt like he had handed me the Holy Grail of teaching! THIS was the secret that I had been after! I did not realize at the time that it was not just a teaching secret that he had shared, but a LIFE secret.

Maintaining a positive attitude is hard. Negative attitudes are relatively easy, especially when we do not consciously cultivate better ones. Think of it like weeding a garden. You have to keep pulling weeds—or in this case, negative thoughts—out so they don't take over.

Think of positive thoughts as flowers. If you weed your garden and pull out the negative thoughts, it allows the positive thoughts to flourish. The more that you pull weeds and water your flowers, the better they grow. However, if you start neglecting your thought garden, those negative thoughts work their way back in again, and the pesky things can take over if left unattended.

The reward for keeping those positive thoughts flourishing is worth the effort. You will be much happier, much more at peace. There will always be things that go wrong, but how you view and react to those things makes a tremendous difference in your happiness level.

"Be the most positive person you know!" the speaker told us. Attitudes are contagious. When you have a negative attitude, it drags everyone around you down, until you all spiral down the toilet bowl together. But when you have a positive attitude, you can almost see little sparks of happiness and inspiration fly.

Second Time's the Charm

When I went back for my second year of teaching, I went back with a positive attitude. It made a world of difference. My students formed better bonds with each other. They got along better, they worked better together, they were happier, and they learned more. Most importantly, I enjoyed my job! I felt like I had stolen some of that pixie dust from the literature teacher down the hall that I so greatly admired.

What could a positive attitude do in your life? It takes work to cultivate it, but the result is worth the effort. Start pulling the weeds of your negative thoughts. They are pesky and you might have a lot to pull at first. Slowly but surely it gets easier, and you will start finding yourself with a smile on your face more and more.

In the next several chapters, I will outline the steps to nurturing a positive attitude, just as I did to prepare for my next year of teaching. Applying this attitude can help you create a better life for yourself and help you become more satisfied with the life you already have.

Chapter 3:

Mindfulness

We all get stressed from time to time, and even the most positive of mindsets can start to waver when we do. As they say: forewarned is forearmed, so I'd like to start our journey toward a better life with some strategies for reducing stress. I want to empower you with the skills to not only develop a positive mindset but to combat those pesky negative thoughts and attitudes.

Mindfulness is a fairly new concept for me. I had never heard the term until I started blogging and spending time on Pinterest. The more I learned about it, the more I liked it. The exercise takes some practice, but I have found it to be an excellent technique to use when I'm feeling stressed.

So... what IS "mindfulness," anyway? Mindfulness is simply being in the moment. It involves processing what is going on around you and taking time to experience what your senses are telling you. Sometimes, I am guilty of being with my family in body, but not in mind. Have you noticed yourself doing that before too? I might be at the park with the kids, but instead of focusing on them, my mind is busy worrying about our finances, or how I'm going to get something done. My mind races from one problem to the next until I have no idea what's happening around me, because instead of experiencing the moment, my mind was a million miles away. I totally missed the park, yet I didn't accomplish anything by worrying.

Mindfulness also helps when I am frustrated or when I feel overwhelmed. I take a few minutes to process all the information that my senses are collecting. It allows me to get more of a bird's eye view of the situation, and to separate my emotions from it. It's hard to make rational decisions when you are overcome with emotion.

What A Mindfulness Exercise Looks Like

As I write this, I am sitting at the dinette in our camper, in the middle of a week-long trip at one of our state parks. I feel the spring of laptop keys as I type and the soft cushion of my seat. My feet are resting on the floor and there is a slight pang in my back that I just noticed because I'm sitting without proper posture. I feel the air conditioner softly ruffling my hair. I hear the voices of my sons. My youngest son is fidgeting and making laps from his bunk to our bed. Their father (my incredible husband) is stretched out on the bed. It is still raining. The tarp we put over the table outside has caught a lot of water, but the campsite is soaking wet.

This exercise made me realize several things:

- I need to stop arching my back when I sit at this table.
- The tarp outside leaks. It needs to be replaced.

But more importantly:

- My husband is a really great dad.
- Despite my reluctance to bring video games camping, they're having some great Father/Sons time.
- I am happy.

- Things may not be perfect, but I am content at this moment.

Mindfulness centers you. The exercise encourages you to pay attention to what is happening, and what you are feeling, in the moment. Like any exercise, it gets easier with practice. It separates you from your emotions so you can better regulate your reactions.

How Mindfulness Has Benefitted Me, and Can Benefit You Too!

As I previously stated, mindfulness takes practice, and I am still perfecting it. I'm sure that as I continue to practice, it will get easier when I am upset. The exercise has already gotten much easier when I am happy and content.

For example, when we went swimming earlier, I did not take my phone. I took exactly zero pictures. However, I had more fun swimming with my family than I've had in quite a while. I wasn't concerned about getting my phone wet, getting the perfect picture, or what time it was. Instead I paid attention to my sensations and feelings: was I hungry, tired, or feeling scared to death about jumping off that tall rock?

I wasn't just an observer worried about what other people would think—I was an active participant. I felt the exhilaration of falling when I jumped into the water. I put on a mask and snorkeled a bit, following two little brim around the rocks for a short time. When my husband swam under me, rolled on his belly like a seal and smiled at me, I laughed. When he tried to kiss me underwater, our facemasks clunked together and I started laughing underwater, spraying bubbles everywhere.

I concentrated on enjoying the moment fully and completely. I wasn't worried about what we were going to have for supper. I wasn't worried about what other people thought. I simply had fun and played with the abandon that my kids so easily enjoy. That is mindfulness to me, and that is living. Worrying steals away the joy of the moment. Don't let it. Be mindful.

Practice, Practice, Practice

Take a minute and do a mindfulness exercise. What do you feel through your skin? Are you hot, cold, just right? Are your feet on the floor, or are you curled up on the couch reading this on your tablet or laptop? What do you hear? What do you see around you?

Now, turn your thoughts inward. Are you worried about anything? Is there something on your mind, distracting you? Are you happy, sad, mad, irritated, exhausted?

This exercise still takes a few minutes for me to do, most likely because I haven't been doing it long, and as you probably noticed in my example, my thoughts still stray. The more I practice, the more I improve, but sometimes I still have to take a few breaths and close my eyes to really center myself on the here and now.

For me, this exercise helps to quiet my worries and focus on what is happening. It may sound crazy, but no one has to know that you're doing it. The next time you're worrying instead of enjoying the moment, take a few deep breaths and try a mindfulness exercise. It will make a difference.

Mindfulness Any Time

Mindfulness is not just for when you are worried about something. I started because I was losing patience with the constant demands on my time once my kids came home for the summer. My whole schedule changed, and I felt like I couldn't get anything done! It was an adjustment for all involved.

I didn't want to be the Mom that yelled all the time. I don't like being angry. It hurts me and it hurts other people. I needed something to help me keep my sanity and my patience. I'm not perfect by any means, but mindfulness is helping, and I am improving. I am building mindfulness muscle! If I can do this, then I know that you can do the same. I believe in you!

Chapter 4:
Letting Go of Worry

Worrying is like a parasite in many ways. It sucks away joy and it keeps us from being present in the moment, as we discussed in the previous chapter.

Before I started researching for this book and my blog, I worried about everything—from what other people thought to bad things that might happen. I was a master "What-ifer." What if such-and-such happens? Or, what if so-and-so doesn't like me? My imagination was constantly consumed with these scenarios. I rationalized that I worried because I cared, so it couldn't be a bad thing, could it? Perhaps if I worried enough about the problem, I could take some of the burden off whomever I was worrying about.

Reading my rationalization now, I see that it makes no sense, but at the time it made perfect sense to me. I thought by worrying I could anticipate problems and cut them off before they happened.

Bottom line is that my worrying stemmed out of insecurity. I was desperate to control everything. Spoiler: life is uncontrollable by nature. We can keep the illusion of control for a little while, like a juggler keeping balls in the air, but sooner or later one of them will fall. Maybe you get tired, maybe your fingers slip, or maybe you get distracted and look away, but inevitably, gravity wins. The illusion of control cannot be kept up indefinitely.

Defining "Worry" and "Concern"

When I googled the definition of worry, it said "give way to anxiety or unease; allowing one's mind to dwell on difficulty or troubles." Give special attention to one word in that definition: **ALLOWING**. Remember, you are in control of your thoughts and feelings, and you must take responsibility for them in order to control them. When you worry, you dwell on difficulty and trouble. Is that the metal state you want to aim for?

In The Power of Self-Coaching: 5 Essential Steps For Creating The Life You Want, Dr. Joseph Luciani made an important distinction between worry and concern when he said, "Worry is incessant, ruminative speculation of what might go wrong; the habit of anticipating chaos." I love the last part: "the habit of anticipating chaos." (We'll come back to that later.) He defines concern as "calculated consideration and assessment of actual danger. More fact-based and geared toward problem solving."

One of those is mentally healthy, the other not so much. I bet you can tell which one is which.

I want you to know that I am not suggesting you shouldn't care. You absolutely should! Caring about yourself and others is healthy. What I want you to avoid is starting down the worry road in the first place. Following that road is like trying on a Chinese finger trap when you might not know how to get out.

If you get stuck in that trap, understanding the difference between worry and concern is one of the first steps to getting out, and will also help you avoid the same trap in the future.

Remember Dr. Luciani's definition up above: concern is based on fact, and is therefore more objective than worry. Concern means that you care. Caring and letting something drive you nuts are two different things, though. Concern is much more mentally healthy than worry because your emotions are proportionate to the situation, and it can even be constructive.

For example, let's say that the tires on my car are getting a bit thin. I always get them inspected when I get my oil changes. They start at 10 mm, so let's say they are at 3 mm right now, and they need to be replaced at 2mm. If I'm concerned about my tires, I can say, "My tires are wearing thin. They need to be replaced soon. I should have about another month, so I'll call a few tire places and see how much it will cost to replace them, and then I will see where I can come up with the money to pay for them."

In this example, my concern is fact-based. My emotions are proportional to the problem, and I am working to solve the problem. It is constructive.

Worrying might look something like this: "Oh no! My tires are thin! What if I get a flat on the freeway? What if there's nowhere to pull over and I have to drive on it until it explodes?! My children might lose their mother in a car crash. My husband would be miserable without his wife. He'd be all alone in this world raising our children by himself! What if he replaces me? He's such a handsome catch that I bet it would not take long! What if she's mean to my kids??! My poor babies!!"

Worry is based on "What if?" scenarios. What if such-and-such happens? What if so-and-so thinks....? Notice there is no evidence to backs up the "what if" problems. "What if" is your imagination running away with you, much the way a child convinces her/himself that there is a monster under his/her bed. My example seemed pretty over the top didn't it? It was not fact based. There was nothing constructive about it, and the emotions were way overblown.

One worry leads to another worry, and before you know it, you're on a runaway worry train. I started with

"My tires are thin" and ended with "I'm dead and my children have an evil step-mother!" Worrying is fiction. It takes a molehill of a problem and turns it into a mountain.

Worrying is Harmful

As I mentioned, I used to worry about pretty much everything. I didn't understand that it was a bad thing, either. I did not understand that this habit was hurting me and everyone around me. A good friend of mine listened to me patiently for at least two years, always telling me "You worry too much!" before I began to see that it was a harmful habit.

I won't get into the negative health effects that worrying can have. I outlined them pretty well in a blog post I wrote on what to do when you worry too much. I have learned some things since I wrote that post, though, and I'd like to share them with you.

What I found most surprising is that avoiding worry has a scriptural basis. Philippians 4:6-7 says

> *"6 Be careful for nothing; but in everything by prayer and supplication with thanksgiving let your requests be made known unto God.*
>
> *7 And the peace of God, which passeth all understanding, shall keep your hearts and minds through Christ Jesus."* (KJV)

The passage hit me like a ton of bricks the first time I read it. It brought me a great deal of comfort, but also stung because I had been wallowing in worry. I didn't realize that my own state of mind was something that I needed to practice controlling. I must have re-read it a half a dozen times. After that, I consciously started working on not worrying so much. The problem was, even though I made some progress, I didn't have concrete strategies for handling worry until recently.

Worrying is a Habit

Think about the Chinese finger trap I mentioned earlier. Have you ever seen one of those? It's a children's toy, made of a flexible woven tube. You put a finger in on either side, but if you try to pull your fingers out quickly, the weaving tightens and your fingers are trapped. The more you pull, the tighter the trap gets. It's very easy to slip into, but hard to get out of – unless you know the secret.

The more you worry, the tighter those worries bind you in the illusion that you cannot escape. The secret to escaping worry and a Chinese finger trap, is the same – you let go. When you stop pulling on the Chinese finger trap, the weaving loosens and you can easily pull your fingers out, one at a time. If you are in a similar trap of worry, I will show you exactly how to let go, so you can once again be free.

Strategies for Managing Worry:

You Can't Fix Everything. Sometimes You Must Let it Go.

The friend I mentioned earlier told me that I could not solve everything, as did my husband. I didn't listen to them at first. I reasoned that if I could just worry enough, care enough, love enough, pray enough, that the problem would go away. That is not the case. There are some problems that you can't fix. Let them go.

- You are not responsible for the choices other people make.

- You are not responsible for the way others react.

- You are not responsible for the feelings that other people choose to focus on.

To you, those three principals might sound like common sense, but they did not always make sense to me. I had to learn and internalize them—a process that I'm still working on. I can't tell you how many times I still repeat those statements to myself. The concept that I was not only responsible for my actions but also for my thoughts and feelings was a new one.

You Are Responsible for Your Own Actions, Thoughts, and Feelings.

Likewise, I knew that my own actions were my choice, but I thought that feelings just happened. I did not realize that I had the choice to control them too. Emotions are HARD to control because they are not rational. Sometimes, like a bunch of monkeys, they try to run wild. However, you have the choice to stop, be mindful, and get them under control. Worrying happens when your monkeys are running wild and it will make you miserable.

Steer Your Thoughts Toward Good Things

It is amazing how we often find exactly what we are looking for. When you focus on your troubles, problems, and worries, they become bigger and bigger until they consume your mind. However, if we start thinking of good things—when we show gratitude and think about all that we are grateful for—we start to see more of those instead. You start feeling happier, you enjoy life more. You also find more good things in your life when you remember to show gratitude. Again, I was astounded to find a scriptural reference to this as well. Philippians chapter 4 states in the 8th verse:

> "8 Finally, brethren, whatsoever things are true, whatsoever things are honest, whatsoever things are just, whatsoever things are pure, whatsoever things are lovely, whatsoever things are of good report; if there be any virtue, and if there be any praise, think on these things." (KJV)

Write Your Thoughts Down in a Journal

I have also found that journaling makes me feel better. Getting my thoughts down on paper helps. Sometimes what I am worried about is personal and not something that I want to talk to other people about, but I can write about them privately. I start by putting those recurring thoughts that are going through my mind on paper. What am I upset about? Who or what is stressing me? What am I feeling right now in this present moment? What do I wish could happen? What do I want to be doing and feeling? I also pray about those private things that worry me. God knows all anyway; I may as well talk to him about it and ask for help. I have done this often enough to know that it works and that I feel better afterward.

Use Breathing Exercises or Visualization to "Change the Channel"

Using visualization to change the channel in your mind is similar to the mindfulness exercise that I described in the previous chapter. Our minds are a constant stream of thoughts, just like the radio is a constant stream of music. What do you do when the station you're listening to starts playing a song you hate? You change the channel! You can visualize and practice doing this with your thought process as well. When you find yourself worrying about something, consciously try to change the channel and think about other things. It will be hard and first and you'll likely find your thoughts moving back what worries you. The exercise gets easier with practice.

If you do not like the "changing the channel" visualization, you can choose something else, like kicking a ball away, boxing out your worries, letting a balloon go, or something else that resonates with you.

Breathing exercises to clear your mind, can help too, but like visualization, it takes practice. Some people refer to these breathing exercises as "meditation," but that term can also go off in other directions as well, so for clarity, I will refer to them as breathing exercises.

Get in a comfortable position and try to clear your mind. I like to picture a black room. Concentrate on your breathing and keeping your thoughts still. Keep that room black. See how long you can maintain the stillness. Your mind is used to wandering, so at first, it will try to run wild. Your goal is to tame those monkeys that are your thoughts, push them away, and redirect your mind once again to blackness. As you practice, you will be able to rest your mind for longer periods of time. If I'm frustrated, I visualize blowing out all the negative thoughts and feelings in black smoke and inhaling love, joy, peace, and happiness. I have also heard of people that prefer to count, or to repeat a good thought, and focus on that. Experiment and find what will work best for you!

Conclusion

Worry is a habit based on insecurity that might give you the illusion of control for a time, but eventually that illusion will shatter because life is unpredictable. Concern is fact-based and constructive, and your emotions will be proportional to the problem that you are facing. Try to be aware of your own thoughts and feelings to decipher which one you might be experiencing, and consider some of the strategies above to combat your worries when they appear.

Getting outside always improves my mental outlook, as does journaling, praying, and focusing on the positive things in my life. Visualization and breathing exercises are both powerful techniques that require practice, but can also be beneficial. I have found all these helpful on my own personal quest for contentment, and I hope that you do too.

Chapter 5:

Why Comparing Yourself to Others Is a Trap

I am naturally competitive. Maybe it comes from being an older sibling. In today's world, athletics are pushed hard, and there is much emphasis placed on being the best, the strongest, the smartest, etc. We see people that have achieved great things and we want to be like them, we want to do the things that they do, and have the things that they have. I get it.

When I was in high school, I wanted to be the smartest kid in my grade at my school. I knew success in athletics was not in the cards for me, so I concentrated on earning the highest A's in all my classes. I wanted the praise and recognition of everyone around me. When I missed a question on a test, I obsessed over it. If I could just learn enough, study hard enough, and be smart enough, I believed I could achieve my goal. No matter how hard I worked, though, I wasn't the absolute best. There was always someone that scored a few points higher than I did while I fell just short of the impossible mark I had set.

I got good grades. I graduated in the top 10% of my class. I accomplished a lot. But I was not the valedictorian, or even the salutatorian. You may be thinking, "Hey, that's pretty good!" But that was not what I saw. I lived in a constant state of struggle, and I was blinded to what I had achieved. Instead, I felt like I had failed.

When you compare yourself to others, it blinds you to what you have accomplished.

Stop Chasing the Carrot

Someone will always be smarter, stronger, faster, have a bigger house, a bigger paycheck, a nicer car, etc. When you compare yourself to others, you trap yourself with an impossible goal, like a cartoon character dangling a carrot in front of his/her horse, just out of reach. You set yourself up for failure. This leads to unease and frustration, and it leaves you feeling that you are not good enough. We become the horse chasing a carrot that will always be just out of reach, no matter how fast we walk. When you compare yourself to others you create a constant sense of "I have to keep up, no matter the cost!" The bar you set is impossibly high. Don't set yourself up for that!

This point was further illustrated for me when I started blogging.

Success Stories

I did research for months before typing up my first few posts. My blogging board on Pinterest was a secret board so that no one would know the crazy idea I was planning. I read about people setting up blogs and growing at a tremendous rate! Thousands of page views, nice incomes—one even made around $100,000...a MONTH! Wowzers! Sign me up, please! As I followed all the free information that I could find and pinned more and more to my secret blogging board on Pinterest, I started to have high hopes.

I set up affiliate links and put ads on the blog. (Most of them are gone now.) I posted things regularly and waited for the traffic and money to roll in, but it didn't. I was working my rear off, but I made a grand total of $1.25 or so from ads, and nothing from my affiliate links.

I can't keep up!

In my blogging groups, I saw new bloggers saying things like "I had 3K page views and made my first $100 in my first month of blogging!" I tried to be happy for them, but I was discouraged. It's not that no one read my blog, because they did—just not in those numbers. The success stories that were once encouraging began to feel like a heavy weight dragging me down. There was no way that I could compete with success stories like that!

I wanted to quit. That is when I knew something had to change.

Change Your Mindset and Stay True to Your Goals

It is amazing how much changing your perspective or your mindset can affect your happiness. I loved blogging, but I knew that if I kept comparing myself to others, I would get so discouraged that I would quit.

I decided to change my mindset. I started focusing on writing and promoting the kinds of posts that I would like to read. I didn't want to read about a blogger that was struggling to make it and only making mediocre progress, at best. I wanted to read encouraging things. I wanted to be lifted up. That's why I started blogging in the first place. I went back to my "why" – the reason I started the blog in the first place.

Instead of my lack of instant progress, I started focusing on my slow-but-steady growth. I stopped checking the statistics every day. I stopped stressing about the slow days, I stopped checking to see how much I had earned through ads or affiliate links. Making money from the blog is not my primary focus. My primary focus is helping people just like you.

I have started seeing positive results. I feel like my content is better quality now and it's much more focused. My page views are up, and I have actually made a little bit of money off of my affiliate links! (Less than $20 at this time, but it's still more than I had before.) When I focus on my personal goals, that's when the growth occurs. The same will hold true for you as well. You will see growth when you focus not on what everyone else is doing, but when you stay true to your purpose.

Contentment Questing is not like any other blog out there. Do you know why? Because it's my blog. No one writes exactly what I write. I won't be everyone's cup of tea. You won't be either, and that's ok. I am not in competition with anyone else, and neither are you.

No One Has A Story Exactly Like Yours

We all face different challenges and come from different backgrounds. I finally realized that most of the success stories I read were from people who had blogged before or, if they were new, they had heavily invested in their blogs, and/or had spent a ton on educating themselves before they launched. They had all the necessary elements for success set up beforehand. They may have made $100 in their first month, but probably invested much more than that from the start.

Contentment Questing is my first blog, and it is very much a learn-as-you-go experience for me. That is ok. I've learned a lot and have accomplished many personal goals. You bring something unique to the table in all your endeavors: yourself. You are an amazing, unique person with unique perspectives and experiences. Being authentically you is much better than trying to mimic someone else.

Steps in Your Quest for Self-Improvement

Document Your Successes

Though I stopped publishing public blog updates that focused on income, page views, and followers every month, as I did for the first 4 months of the blog, I do still keep track of my progress. It's encouraging! Document your improvements. For personal successes, I keep a journal. For the blog, I update the follower tabs monthly, and I have a plug-in that tracks page views and visitors. There are times my stats dip, but overall there is a growth trend, so I try not to get too discouraged. There will always be ups and downs in everything that you do. The important thing is that you keep going. Persistence will pay off in the end.

Hold Yourself Accountable

Set goals for yourself and write them down. You're more likely to see it through that way. Something about seeing it on paper makes you more likely to remember them and follow through.

Once you set your goals, hold yourself accountable. If you set goals and forget about them, they do not serve much of a purpose other than temporarily making you feel good about yourself. This is why that SMART goals have a time frame.

We will cover goal-setting with more detail in a later chapter. For now, set aside a time to review your goals. The end or beginning of the month is a good time for general purpose goal review.

So, how do you hold yourself accountable? Different people have different techniques. I have tried several myself--for example, writing them down in my journal and reviewing them at the end of the month. I have also shared them in Facebook groups, and tried having an accountability partner. What works best for me is just writing them down in my journal and having an accountability partner (usually my husband.) When I shared my goals in Facebook groups, I often ended up forgetting what I wrote. Tami, who blogs at theinspirationlady.com, shares her monthly goals on her blog at the beginning of the month and also publicly evaluates how she did on her goals from the previous month.

In short, find what works best for you, and try to see it through.

Celebrate Small Successes and Reward Yourself

This is so important for your overall happiness. When you hold yourself accountable and document your small successes, it emphasizes your accomplishments. Celebrate them!

Large successes are a sum of the small ones. When you reach a goal, it gives you positive feedback, and so does the celebration. When you get positive feedback, you are more inclined to continue your progress, and in turn you reach more goals. This becomes a positive feedback loop that feeds your self-confidence!

It is ok to modify your goals if you are not reaching them. What matters is picking yourself up and trying again. Keep going and don't quit!

Conclusion

You are special and unique, and you bring things to the table that no one else does, simply because you are you. Instead of comparing yourself to others, change your perspective and focus on your personal growth. Stay true to your purpose, whatever that may be. You can and will do amazing things!

Chapter 6:
Self-Care

What is self-care and why is it important?

The name seems petty self-explanatory: it means caring for yourself. What's amazing is that such a simple concept can be so hard to put into practice. I have often seen the analogy of "put your own oxygen mask on first" in regards to self-care. Depending on your circumstance you may or may not struggle with this.

When I was first married and it was just me and my husband, self-care was not really an issue. I took care of him, I took care of me, and that was it. We worked together to do the things that needed done around the house. Once we had our first child, though—then I learned quickly just how exhausted a person can be and still keep moving. "Mombie" (Mom Zombie) became the norm for me, since I was the one staying home with the baby. That is when I started to realize the importance of self-care. To put it in scientific terms, the importance of self-care is directly proportional to your stress level, so if you feel exhausted and ready to explode that's when you need self-care the most.

Most of my self-care examples are Mom examples from my own life, but the principles apply no matter your situation. When you are giving of yourself, you first must be sure that you have something to give.

Mom Life

When I became a mother, the focus of my life suddenly shifted and began to revolve around both my husband and the new baby, instead of just the two of us. A mother's primary job revolves around caring for other people. We respond to the needs of our children no matter when they need us. Baby waking up multiple times a night? Don't worry, sweetheart, Momma's here. Kindergartener throwing up in bed in the middle of the night? Mom is there, too. Middle of the day and someone needs a snack and a nap? Mom is there providing for her kids. Husband comes home after a horrible day? That's in our domain as well.

What about a shower for ourselves? Depending on the age of your children, you might be thinking, "ah yes, that's so relaxing once the kids are at school!" Or you might be thinking, like I did, "Yes! I'm a champion at that Olympic sport. You know, the one when you have people screaming your name and you are trying to finish in the fastest time possible?"

All those examples involve giving—giving of yourself, your time, your emotions, your energy, and often your sleep. If your job is to give and take care of others, how can you fulfill that role if you have nothing left? How can you give when you are totally depleted? We scrape the bottom of the bucket and we come up with some hidden strength when push comes to shove, but how much better are your gifts to your family when your bucket is full?

Probably much better. For example, if your gas tank is approaching empty, you stop and fill it up. Why do we hesitate to do the same for ourselves? When we make the time for self-care, we are more productive, less stressed, and more prepared to give. When we do not take the time for self-care, we wind up doing things that are less healthy, like stress eating (guilty!) and binge-watching tv.

Making Time for Self-Care When You're Overwhelmed

I'm going to say that the most common reason that we neglect self-care is that we feel there is no time. We have so many responsibilities. Other people are depending on us to pull it all together, and we might believe failure is not an option. We get so focused on accomplishing our tasks and caring for our little ones that self-care is continually shoved to the back burner.

I might tell myself: I'll sit down when I get X done. In the middle of the task I am trying to accomplish, though, something else comes up, and the original task ends up taking much longer than expected because I'm trying to do two things at once. Time for myself never quite happens. Before I know it, bedtime rolls around, and instead of going to bed I'm looking at "one more thing" on the internet, trying to unwind a bit. Taking "me time" instead of sleep time never works very well for me, so I end up just as exhausted and stressed as ever. Does this ever happen to you? Does it ever seem like there are not enough hours in the day to finish what you need to get done and also take much-needed time for yourself?

You Are Worth Investing In

I will share a secret: you have time to do what you MAKE time for. Does that seem odd? It's about prioritizing. My friend, YOU are worth making time for. You are important, how you feel is important, and your wants and your needs matter. Think of these statements as virtual hugs and embrace them!

The people that you so lovingly serve need you, which means they also need you to keep your sanity. They need a version of you that is not worn ragged and at the end of his/her rope. Go do something that you love. It might only last 20 minutes, but you need that break like you need oxygen and food. That emotional recharge time will refill your bucket so you can go back to being the amazing person that you are.

Set aside a certain time each day that you will not spend working. For me, it was nap time when my kids were still small. For you, it might be early in the morning before your kids wake up, or it might be in the evenings after they go to bed. No matter what is happening, that is YOUR time. Make it a priority and remember that by taking care of yourself, you are also taking care of your family.

Types of Self-Care

Self-care is not all bubble baths and candles. (But those are nice!) Self-nurturing activities can fall into five categories: Sensory, Emotional, Spiritual, Physical, and Social. (Kathrine Hurst wrote an article on self-care that gives a great break-down of this concept.)

Sensory Self-Care

Have you ever tried to sleep at night and were extremely tired, but your mind kept you awake and staring at the ceiling? I know that I have. You might be ready to quit for the day, but your brain is wrestling with everything you've been stressing about, too stimulated to rest well. Different people have different tolerances for what is overstimulating, but I think at some point it can be overwhelming for anyone.

If you need to calm your mind down, do something that falls into the sensory self-care category: try lighting a candle with your favorite scent, brewing a cup of hot tea, putting on some relaxing music, or closing your eyes and snuggling under a blanket. Try to stop and savor the moment for a little while, and focus on what you feel using your five senses. Take deep breaths and soak everything in. You might also try some breathing exercises or a mindfulness exercise here as well. I have found that both help to calm my mind at the end of a long day.

Doing something that you loved before you were a mom also fits in the sensory self-care category. For example, if you earned a living from painting prior to becoming a mom, you might try setting up a time to paint. If you were a writer before, then you might try blogging or writing an eBook. If you enjoyed playing the piano, take time for that. Whatever hobby you choose, the important thing is that it unwinds your mind, engages your senses, and gives you joy.

Emotional Self-Care

If I am upset about something, I cannot focus or have fun until I deal with whatever emotion is bothering me. It might be tempting to think of emotions as "good" or "bad," but in reality, they are neither. It is ok to not be happy all the time, and it's healthy to let yourself acknowledge and deal with those emotions. Dealing with them is actually much better than suppressing your feelings, because it allows you to process them and then let them go.

When you take an emotion and figuratively shove it in the closet, that closet door will occasionally open when you feel overwhelmed, and everything will come tumbling out, which forces you to deal with it over and over again. Let yourself acknowledge the emotion, and then move on if it is not one that you need to keep. Think of this as decluttering your emotional closet.

When you need to exercise emotional self-care, consider seeking out a family member that you really feel understands you. Talking through your emotions with your husband or close friend might help, or journaling, listening to music that reflects your emotional state, or letting yourself have a good cry if you need one. I like an activity that lets me think things through. For example, some of my best thinking is done while in the shower or on a brisk walk.

Spiritual

I look forward to going to church each Sunday because it recharges me. Listening to the sermon reminds me how much my heavenly Father loves me. It reminds me to be grateful for the blessings in my life, and that the trials I'm going through are just temporary. Going to church puts my life in perspective. That is part of my spiritual self-care. Another part of my spiritual self-care is taking time to pray alone, usually in silence. There is something healing and restoring about it because that's the time that I talk to my Heavenly Father about all that's all on my heart. It makes me feel more connected to Him.

Gratitude is something we should all practice. We all have blessings that we take for granted. Sometimes pausing to read scripture or thinking about the things that we are grateful for, or even journaling about them, can bring great peace.

Physical

Don't run away yet! (But even if you do, it counts as self-care!) Our bodies need physical exercise. Humans aren't meant to sit in one place all day. When we work out, our bodies release a natural feel-good chemical called endorphins, which helps melt away stress (and fat!) and leaves you with more energy, and also a better mood.

However, physical self-care is not just about exercise. It can also include going to the doctor when you are sick, making sure that you have the right prescription glasses or contacts if you need them, and making sure that you take care of your teeth. You need to be healthy in order to take care of everyone else. If you would take your kids to the doctor for what's bothering you, then you probably need to take yourself as well.

One of my favorite forms of physical self-care is going for a walk outside. I used to take my kids with me when they were little, either in a backpack, a wrap, or a stroller. When my youngest son was little, he had a balance bike that he STILL loves. He had no problem keeping up with me on our walk. I got some self-care, and he burnt off some extra energy! Win-win.

Social

When I transitioned from full-time high school teacher to stay-at-home mom, one of the greatest challenges was the lack of people contact. Before, I talked to a hundred people a day. Once I became a mom, I had only my newborn son (who was not much of a conversationalist at the time) and my husband to talk to. My parents were close, and I talked to them about every other day, but I was still going through a serious lack of social time! Cue the Little Mermaid song "I want to be where the people are." It was hard to adjust, especially since my car's engine had blown up a few weeks before I gave birth, and I was pretty much stuck at the house.

I quickly learned the value of a good friend! I was so grateful when my friends called to talk. It cheered me up immensely. I also made another mommy friend around the time my son was 7 months old, who I am still good friends with today. I lived for playdates, and I think she did too.

We always ended up staying longer than we meant to because it was so nice to talk to another mommy!

If this is where you are, find your tribe. Find people that will support you. (More on that in Chapter 13.) Make time for talking with your husband. Make time for calling that friend that you haven't talked to in forever. I think women, especially, benefit from social interaction. Life was not meant to be lived in isolation.

Conclusion

What are your self-care challenges? Is it making time for yourself, figuring out what to do for yourself, or something else? Remember that you have to take care of yourself and fill your own bucket first before you can fill those of all the people that you love and take care of. You are important, you are loved, and your wants, needs, and feelings matter! We are in this together, so let's help one another!

Chapter 7:
The Power of Gratitude

Another great way to take care of yourself is with the power of gratitude. It's not like "the power to fly" or "the power to snap your fingers and have an instantly clean house" (I want that one! Sign me up please!), or "the power to do 3 things at once." It may sound silly at first, but gratitude is powerful because it shifts your mindset.

We all fall into the self-pity trap from time to time. Gratitude is how we pull ourselves out. Self-pity focuses on what we don't have, or what we wish we had. Gratitude, on the other hand, is giving thanks and remembering what we DO have. Yes, there are things that I want, but on the other hand there are things that I take for granted that I know I would be devastated without.

The value of gratitude is not in the making of a list. **The real value of gratitude is how it shifts our mindset.**

Count Your Blessings

When I am feeling sad, upset, sorry for myself, or angry, I am usually focusing on what is wrong with ME or MY life. You can get so wrapped up in what is going on with you and your family, so trapped in your own little world, that you forget to look outside of it. Empathizing with other people takes emotional energy, and sometimes you might not feel that you have enough.

The amazing thing is, when you start counting your blessings, the list gets longer and longer the more that you think about what is going right instead of what's going wrong. Here's another amazing thing: the list never ends because there is always something new to be grateful for. Many of these blessings are small, but small things often add up to make a big difference.

Starting a gratitude list might be hard at first, especially if your state of mind is similar to what I described above. It gets easier with practice. Also, don't be discouraged if your gratitude list looks much the same from day to day. That's a GOOD thing, because it means that some of the blessings that you had yesterday are continuing through today. I'll give some more specific advice on that later on in the chapter.

The definition of gratitude is remembering your blessings and giving thanks for both the little things and the big ones. When the amazing becomes common place you start to take it for granted. Start counting your blessings and find your gratitude once again.

Everyday Blessings

I see my husband every day. I cook dinner for him (or we go out) every night. I talk with him, coordinate life with him. I love him. While this probably sounds pretty ordinary, if you stop and think about it, the situation is quite amazing. First, among all the people in the world, we found each other. I used to think that my Prince Charming was lost in the desert somewhere, or had taken a wrong turn before finding me, but it turns out he was just in a neighboring town!

My husband is the person I talk to the most. He understands me. He knows all my faults, and he's seen me at my absolute worst, and yet he still loves me unconditionally! I have a partner in life that I can lean on and depend on to help me. I would be devastated without him.

But not all everyday blessings are that life-changing. I mentioned cooking for him; that means we have the money to buy food. I have electricity to cook it with, and a house to cook it in. We have clean, running water in the house. I have amazing devices that keep food cold or frozen, and others that can heat it up with the push of a button! Sometimes, when all those amazing gadgets and plentiful food are still not enough, we go out and buy food that has already been prepared—which means that we also have transportation and fuel.

All of these are everyday blessings that I often take for granted, but when I stop and break them down like that... wow! That's pretty powerful.

What Are You Grateful For?

Set aside two minutes and find a clean sheet of paper. Write down some of the things that you're grateful for. Go ahead—I'll wait for you, I promise.

If you are having trouble getting started, think of the last thing that made you smile. Who (or what) was it? Did your dog do something really goofy? Did your cat come and lay down on your hands as you were trying to type? Maybe your cat missed a jump, landed in a heap and then walked away with an "I meant to do that!" expression? Did your child smile at you? Did they offer you a hug? Maybe they said something really cute. Did you have a really nice conversation with your Mom or a friend? Were you able to sit down with a nice, hot cup of coffee or tea this morning? Are you wearing your favorite fuzzy socks? Will you watch your favorite show on Netflix tonight?

Whatever it was that you just thought about, start your list or your paragraph with that. Be specific, relax and just let the thoughts flow, like you are following a stream or a spaghetti noodle. As an example, I will go with "nice, hot cup of coffee this morning."

- Coffee – hot, smells great, warms all the way down, wakes me up.
- Caffeine – makes me feel ready to face the day. Puts my brain on go.
- Keurig – instant gratification (and coffee), so easy. Best Valentine's Day gift ever!
- Hot shower.
- Fluffy towel.
- Steam – breaks up congestion in my nose. I can breathe!
- Clean clothes – broken in jeans, my favorite sweatshirt, comfy sneakers.
- Thankful that I can wear jeans and sweatshirt on weekdays.
- Make-up – I feel pretty today, and comfy!
- Pony tail holders – thank goodness since hair is a big poof ball today.
- Toothbrush – love teeth feeling clean.
- Mouthwash – small thing that was a "luxury" item when I was a kid.
- Clean mouth.
- Good teeth – so glad I didn't have to suffer through braces.
- Smile – I really like my smile. Hope it brightens someone else's day, too.

As you can see, everything that I listed was a very ordinary, small thing. By thinking about each little thing and acknowledging it, each little thing that I would normally take for granted makes me smile when I stop long enough to give thanks for it.

How is your own list looking? Do you feel any differently than you did before? I hope the answer is yes. If not, keep thinking and writing. Try taking time each day to remember what you are grateful for and to give thanks. Some people keep a gratitude journal, but any place that suits you is fine. Other people write theirs in a planner, or on sticky notes that they put where they will see them. I have also heard of keeping a gratitude jar, so you can pull the little pieces of paper out to read when you feel down. Try practicing this once a week and see if you notice a shift in your emotional and mental state.

But what if your list looks the same every day? I could write the example list pretty much any ordinary morning. Don't worry: it's ok if your list looks the same! Who said that you need to have different blessing each day to be happy? As I mentioned, the power of the gratitude exercise is not the list itself. However, if you find that the same list is not making you any happier, start it with something different that makes you smile. You can also focus on one thing or person and remind yourself WHY you are thankful for them.

For example, I'm thankful for my house. It makes me happy. If I sit down and focus on why, my list might look like this:

- My own space
- Cute
- Blue (my favorite color)
- Big yard
- Garden spot
- Close to walking track and creek
- Nice neighbors
- Love the mirror in the living room as I walk in
- Walls are NOT Pepto-Bismol pink, as they were when we moved in.
- 2 bathrooms! (One of them we recently added on)
- Kids have separate bedrooms
- Love view from my desk out the window
- Love the window over the kitchen sink that looks out into the yard
- Comfy couch
- Walk in closets
- Working washer and dryer (laundromat is a pain)
- My creative/happy space
- Bookshelves filled with books
- Patch on roof is holding and not leaking

I could go on, but I'll stop here. Just let one thought flow into another. I have also found it helpful, if I'm totally drawing a blank, to do something else for a while that occupies my hands or body while I think about what to write. I might clean house for a bit, or empty the dishwasher, feed the cat, take out the trash, run an errand, go for a walk, etc. This gives me time to mull it over and makes the search less frustrating. If you are still having trouble getting started, then go do something else for a bit and try to remember the last thing that made you smile, or think about a major blessing in your life.

I Hate Lists! That's Too Much Work. What Can I Do Instead?

Sometimes, instead of making lists, I focus on one thing each day. I am doing that on my Facebook page for the month of November. Have you seen the "Thirty Days of Thankful" challenge? You're supposed to write something that you are thankful for on your status each day for a month. If you don't want to do a list, or don't have time for a list, then just write down one thing each day for a month. Try a week at first, if a month seems too long.

I find that, when I try to find one thing each day for a certain period of time, I start LOOKING for things to be grateful for. Sometimes I find more than one thing that I want to put on my status for a given day.

For example, today I stopped and noticed the sunrise. On many days, I'm so busy thinking about what I need to accomplish that I just rush past without thinking or really looking. Today I noticed the sunrise, and I called my sons' attention to it, too. Not only was I able to see a brilliantly painted sky, but I was able to share it with two of the people that I love most in the world. Later in the morning, I also realized that one of my friends was celebrating a birthday today. I started thinking about how different my life would have been without her in it. So, this morning, I came up with enough for two days of Facebook status posts. By tomorrow, I'm sure that I will come up with at least two more.

As mentioned earlier, there is the practice of keeping a gratitude jar, or a thankful jar. You just set it on the table, and when you think of something you are thankful for, you jot it down on a strip of paper and put it in the jar. Some people do this for a month, and other people go on for longer, like several months or a year. At the end of the month, or whatever period of time you set, you open the jar and read the strips of paper, either to yourself or as a family activity.

Other people just write down a few things that they are grateful for in a bullet journal at the end of the day. If you know that you are going to write those three things down before you go to sleep, then you spend the day looking for them.

If you are still stuck or would like a bit of a boost, I have a 30 days of gratitude prompts printable in my freebie library that should get you off to a good start. You can either enter your email address in the box for access, or email me at jennifer@contentmentquesting.com, and I'll be happy to send it to you.

Conclusion

Often, we find what we are looking for. If we're looking for what has gone wrong, that's what we see. On the other hand, if we are looking for things that have gone right or that we are grateful for, we usually find those too.

There is no "right" or "wrong" way to practice gratitude. Find what works for you. The most important part of the practice is the shift in our frame of mind. The mind is a powerful thing—it can make us absolutely miserable, or make us so happy that we feel we are not just living day-to-day, but living an abundant life.

Chapter 8:
Self-Talk

It's no accident that gratitude has such a profound impact on our mindset. Many parts of mindset (and attitude) boil down to what is referred to as "self-talk" in the personal development niche. It's exactly what it sounds like: most of the time, self-talk is what we tell ourselves—mentally, not out loud.

We all have an inner dialogue. Sometimes it can be a force for good, such as when we practice gratitude, but at other times what our inner voice says is not very nice. Like me, you may be all too familiar with the moment that inner voice becomes something else: the inner critic.

The Inner Critic

Contentment Questing's launch was accidental. I thought hitting the "publish" button would give me a preview of what the completed post would look like. Not so, and I didn't know how to un-do what I had done! I was literally shaking, but I had a couple of posts ready, so I published them too, and then I went for a walk to clear my head.

"What have you done?" The voice in my head demanded as I reached the mailbox. "You put something out there on the internet for anyone to read. Just who do you think you are anyway? Who's going to want to read that crap you put out there? You're no expert. You're just a stay at home mom that doesn't know anything. You are a big fraud. People are going to discover that, you know. People are going to realize that you are just pretending. You are making yourself look like a fool. This is going to end in disaster and it's going to be all YOUR fault!"

Wow. That's rather harsh, isn't it? There is no way that I would ever talk to a friend like that. Yet, that's how my inner critic spoke to me. If this conversation has a familiar ring to it, you are not alone. Psychologists refer to these thoughts as "Automatic Negative Thoughts" (ANTs), and they also call the inner critic a "sub-personality." You are not crazy.

When I see an ant, my first reaction (assuming they are not fire ants) is to squash a few with my finger. It's strangely satisfying. Then, if I see a trail of them, I break out the bug spray or the ant bait. Automatic Negative Thoughts (ANTs) can be dealt with much the same way as the insects that they call to mind.

Just as insects have a queen at the center of their hive, our ANTs also have a "queen" and her name is Insecurity. She's pretty tough, and you probably will not completely defeat her. She will still rear her ugly head from time to time, but that does not mean that you have to submit to her reign. I'm going to show you how to overthrow her, so you can rule your own life.

Squashing ANTs

I mentioned that the first thing that I do when I see a single ant is squash it. When you first hear your inner critic start whispering things that make you feel bad and bring you down, squash it with the truth. Your inner critic is a liar, and nothing dismantles a lie faster than the truth. The things that your inner critic whispers are all based on insecurity.

When my inner critic started to pound me with a monologue of negative thoughts after I launched my blog, I started squashing those ANTs with the truth. In answer to "What have you done?" I said, "I started a blog." I tried something new. I stretched the boundaries of my comfort zone, which is always a bit uncomfortable, but that's how we grow. Lots of people have blogs. Some are just hobbies, some turn into businesses, but everyone that writes a blog enjoys it. There is too much work involved in upkeep if you don't.

In answer to "You put something out there on the internet for anyone to read. Who do you think you are, anyway? You are just a stay at home mom that doesn't know anything," I said yes, I DID put a few articles on the internet for anyone to read. Some may like them and some may not, but I am not responsible for other people's reactions. If they don't like what I wrote, they do not have to continue reading, and will most likely navigate a way. Big deal.

Yes, I am a stay at home mom. I'm also a person that has some life experiences. I have a college degree. I taught school and had the privilege of teaching and meeting some amazing teens. I am a mother to two amazing sons, and I am the wife of Prince Charming. I have value. Maybe I can use what I know to do some good. Perhaps, it will help me along the way as well.

My inner critic also said, "You are a big fraud. People are going to discover that, you know. People are going to realize that you are just pretending. You are making yourself look like a fool. This is going to end in disaster and it's going to be all YOUR fault!" However, I know I'm not pretending. I am real and authentic on my blog. I perhaps reveal too much about my inner thoughts there, but other people are struggling with the same things that I am. Maybe we can help each other. I need to broaden my world and make friends. I hope people discover me!

Trying to help people live a happier, better life, or to enjoy the one they have, is not foolish. It's actually quite wise. You only get one shot at life, right? I'm going to do all the good I can, when I can. Worst case scenario is that no one reads the blog, and I will not be any worse off than I am now. So what? The only thing I have to lose is time. I'm going to enjoy the journey and learn something from this experience.

As you can see, ANTs crumble quickly when exposed to the truth. Those lies are meant to tear you down. They are mean to make you bow your head low and to keep you from trying. Don't let them succeed. Stop and analyze what they are telling you. Do you hear truth or fiction?

My walk could have gone several ways that day, with the fate of Contentment Questing in the balance. Had I succumbed to my inner critic and her army of ANTs, I would have come back defeated, and my blog would have stopped before it began. I would have been too scared to try. But I didn't stop. I can't say that I knew what I was doing at the time, because at that point I had not heard anything about ANTs, or how to handle the inner critic, and I was just starting my personal development journey. I wasn't an expert yet, but I was determined to learn.

How to Send Queen Insecurity Running

That day, I won the battle. But the war with Queen Insecurity is far from over. To defeat the Queen, you have to win many battles. That may mean changing your habits. Letting the Inner Critic rule our lives and talk down to us can become a habit. If you are used to tearing yourself down all the time with "I can't do that" thoughts or beliefs, they limit you, and you become comfortable with those limits.

Eventually, that self-talk becomes a set of limiting beliefs. The danger with limiting beliefs is that our thoughts form our beliefs, and our beliefs influence our actions. It's a linked chain. To start our "battle plan" against Queen Insecurity, let's take a look at how we talk to ourselves.

First, let's answer a few questions:

- What thoughts to you think to yourself on a normal basis?

For example, do you tell yourself "I don't know enough to do that?" Or do you choose to say, "I can learn"? Do you think "I could never do what so and so does"? Or do you think "I really like what so-and-so does. What steps did they take to get there? I can do that too."

- How do those thoughts make you feel? Do you feel empowered to try something, or are you scared to try?

- Do the thoughts that you think to yourself tear you down or build you up?

Take a minute and jot down your answers so you have them ready for the next step.

Why What you Think to Yourself Matters

Before continuing with this exercise, I'd like to take a minute and tell you why it matters. Our brains are amazing. The more I learn about how the brain works, the more in awe I am. How we talk to ourselves can be viewed like a computer program that the mind runs. The input that we give our brains matter because it forms the basis for our beliefs, and as I stated above, our beliefs affect our actions (or lack thereof.)

So, if I tell myself over and over again, "I can't remember names," "I'm too dumb to do that," "I'm not fast enough," or "I'm not talented enough," my brain starts believing this internal program to be true, and it tries to carry out the program to make it reality. Have you ever told yourself, "I can't remember names. I'm not going to be able to remember a single name of anyone in the room when I leave this event." Sure enough, you get in there, and go through introductions, and when you leave, you cannot name a single person you just met? You trained your brain to forget it. Like dragging files to the Recycling Bin on your PC, you told your brain that's irrelevant information. As a result, your brain deleted it!

On the other hand, what if you told yourself, "I'm great at remembering names, and I'm going to make my best effort to remember everyone's name that I am introduced to today?" When you leave the event, you have a much higher chance of recalling at least some of the names with that mindset. You won't recall everything perfectly, because skills like this take practice, but you will have some degree of success, which will in turn build your confidence.

I actually tried this exercise. Before I learned that the brain works this way, I had been telling myself for years that I'm not all that good at names. I said, "I know I will forget their name as soon as I am introduced. It's going to be so embarrassing!" (It was.)

After hearing about this, when I saw some new people show up at church, I told myself "I'm good at remembering names. I'm going to introduce myself and I'm going to remember their names, and call them by name if they show up next week." My thoughts influenced my actions: when I introduced myself, I paid better attention than I usually did and employed visualization techniques to help me remember. For example, if the man had said "I'm Mark," I would have envisioned a big red check mark on his forehead. If the woman had said "I'm Karen," I would have imagined a big pink heart. (CARE-en). I also used their name within 5 seconds of being told what it was. "Mark, I'm so pleased to meet you. I'm really glad you came today." If I had remained convinced that I could not remember names, I would not have employed those memory tricks.

When I was asked what their names were after church, I was able to recall them with reasonable accuracy. There were still some that I forgot, but my success gave me confidence.

Identifying and Changing Your Limiting Beliefs

Now that you know why it matters, let's take another look at those limiting beliefs. Did you get anything written down? If you had trouble coming up with answers, think about something you really want to do, and then ask what might be either holding you back, or encouraging you to try.

Think about how your beliefs influence your actions. Write that down beside it. Then, ask what you could start saying to yourself to contradict that limiting belief, and the resulting actions you could start taking. For my example above, my page would look something like this:

> **Limiting Belief:** I can't remember anyone's name to save my life.
>
> **How it influences my actions:** I don't introduce myself to people for fear of not remembering their names and being embarrassed. When I am introduced to someone, I forget their name almost immediately. I don't try very hard to remember it, either. There's no point.
>
> **Statement to Contradict Limiting Belief:** I am good with names. I will remember people's names the next week after being introduced to them.
>
> **Actions I Could Take to Support New Statement:** I know several memory techniques that I have not been using. When introduced to someone, I can pay better attention to their name in the first place. I can also use their name by saying "Nice to meet you, (name)!" That will let me hear the name a second time. I can also use visualization strategies to help me remember their name. The mental image will help to jog my memory.

The "statement to contradict (my) limiting belief" is also known as an affirmation. These are statements we make that we generally want to be true of ourselves, or that directly conflict a limiting belief. They are the "new program" that we want our brain to run, and our subconscious to carry through on. I actually went through a free 3 day mindset reset training that helped me to identify my limiting beliefs and craft affirmations for myself that helped in my personal journey. It was all done through email and pdfs, but I still keep them to reference.

I will be the first to admit, that it sounds funny at first to tell yourself these things. In fact, it's often downright strange. These statements help build you up and help to modify those beliefs that are holding you back. Try repeating them to yourself every day for a week and see if you feel better. They work best when you come up with your own so they can be custom tailored to contradict your own personal limiting beliefs. I keep mine in a journal that I try to read often. It may also help to say them aloud. There is something about not only seeing your affirmations, but also hearing them, that makes them more believable.

Conclusion

How you talk to yourself matters a great deal. It can either tear you down with criticism rooted in insecurity, or it can lift you up and empower you to overcome your own limiting beliefs. The first step in combating insecurity and limiting beliefs is identifying them. The second is to craft statements (or affirmations) that contradict them. By themselves, your thoughts may not seem like that much of a big deal, but they influence your actions. Combat your inner critic with truth and start squashing those ANTs when they creep up on you.

Chapter 9:

Dealing with the Past and Pushing Through Hard Times

Life is often not easy, nor should it be. There is not one person I know who has not gone through tough times. As much as we would like to, we cannot control life. You may have the illusion of control for a time, but something will come along and shatter that illusion.

Such moments of weakness do not define us, and we should not allow ourselves to be victimized by them. Do not let worry rob you of your happiness. Remember that each challenge is an opportunity for personal growth.

Challenges Created by Our Choices

Each day we are confronted by tons of choices. Some are quite easy like "What will I wear today?" while some of them are harder, like "Should I move across the nation for a new job?" Some of these choices have a huge impact on our lives. For example, I decided to NOT marry the loser I was dating before my husband and moved on. I said "yes" and "I do" to my husband. I had a career based on the choice of college degrees I made, and we are living in the house that we decided to purchase. Each of these was a choice under our control.

Obviously, not all of our choices will work out perfectly. If some of your choices did not work out quite the way you hoped, it does not mean all is lost.

We can always work to change the circumstances that we are in. Often, this requires hard work, patience, and commitment, but change is possible. Remember that these challenges are opportunities for personal growth, so it is important to look forward to the future instead of lamenting the mistakes of yesterday.

Challenges of Circumstance

Sometimes the unexpected happens. These events can be minor, but sometimes they are not so minor—like the unexpected death of a loved one, or an act of nature like your house getting struck by lightning. Sometimes we find ourselves in circumstances that are challenging and it seems there is no way out.

To handle these challenges, you must trust in your own ability to handle your own life. The Lord sometimes uses these circumstances to help us grow. That means that He uses the challenge to strengthen you, teach you, or change you in some way that will benefit you later on.

When we first decided to start taking care of an elderly relative, the initial adjustment was tough. Sometimes it is still tough, because I am juggling more "balls." However, I knew from the start that this situation would be an opportunity for personal growth. The experience still challenges me, but I can already tell that some good is coming out of it. For example, my patience has improved, and I can better deal with my emotions and those of everyone around me.

Just like all of us, I am a work in progress. I find it helpful to remember that while it may be a temporary pain in the tail, it will pass and things will get better.

Victimhood

I realize that sometimes events in our lives are totally outside our control, and I will not deny that bad things happen to good people. What I am referring to as "victimhood" is a state of mind: the feeling that the world owes us something because we have been wronged. It allows us to maintain the illusion of control and frees us of responsibility.

Occupying this mentality is a CHOICE that we make. We might make this choice out of habit, or perhaps unconsciously, but it is still a choice. The mentality of victimhood allows a bad thing or circumstance define our lives.

In, his book "The Walk," Richard Paul Evans says "We can spend our days bemoaning our losses or we can grow from them. Ultimately, the choice is ours. We can be victims of circumstance or masters of our own fate, but make no mistake… we cannot be both." Victimhood steals our freedom by allowing someone or something else determine the course of our lives. Our most important life lessons come from adversity (or as Lisa Nichols says, that sometimes the best gifts come "wrapped in sandpaper"). Some of the people I find most inspiring, including the authors I mentioned above, began their stories in adversity. Like a mythical phoenix, they have both risen from ashes. You can too.

If you are going through a difficult time in your life instead of asking "Why me?" ask, "What can I learn from this?" or "How can this help to shape me into a better person?"

Tough times are not fun, but they're an unavoidable part of life. Sometimes these difficulties are a result of our choices, but just as often, they are outside of our control. You can either worry about the unavoidable, or you can trust yourself to handle it.

How to Use Challenges to Grow

Nothing makes me stop and examine myself more than when life presents a challenge. When I'm not comfortable I want things to change, and I want them to change NOW! But sometimes you have to be a bit uncomfortable to find inspiration for change, or even to realize that something needs to change. When I am sitting comfortably in a chair, for example, it's hard to find the motivation to get up and move. Life is like that too. If we are comfortable all the time, we likely will never try anything new or try to challenge ourselves. This is a one good reason to view challenges as opportunities for personal growth.

Prayer

When I go through a rough time, one of the first things it should inspire me to do is seek a closer relationship with God. I will admit, however, that sometimes it takes me far too long to start. I stubbornly continue to think, "It's ok, I can handle this," and I try to rely on my own strength. Often, I won't give up until things keep going wrong and I have more stress on my shoulders than I feel I can bear.

In life, a lesson is repeated until it is learned. I'm not saying that I don't pray when those rough times hit—I do. However, when my back is against the wall and I have nowhere left to turn, I pray harder, I read more, and I seek comfort, just like the child that runs and has no time to hug his mother until he falls and scrapes his knee. Then he comes as fast as he can run to Mom.

Like that small child, the more we run to God for comfort when we are hurting, the more our relationship with Him is built. Hopefully, that means that we want to please him and do what is right. But even if we don't, God is always there for us just like that child's mother (or Father), and he loves his children unconditionally. It comforts me greatly to know that there is no way I can mess up so badly that God can't fix it. No matter how bad things get, I know that it's going to work out.

Gratitude

There is nothing like losing something that is precious to you to make you feel grateful for what you already have. Gratitude is a popular word right now, but it's not new. Gratitude has been around for a very long time.

So often the most precious things are the ones we take for granted because they are always here. For example, when my car's engine blew up, shortly before giving birth to my oldest son, I was extremely thankful that we still had one very old, quirky, working car. When we were able to get a new car, I silently gave thanks for it every time I walked out, loaded the carseat, and went somewhere. Practice gratitude daily, especially when life challenges you, like we talked about in chapter seven. It shifts your mindset from what you are going through to the blessings in your life that are always there.

Compassion

Practicing random acts of kindness makes us feel good inside. What is easily forgotten is how much it can mean to the person that receives it. Some time back, I was feeling down—sad and overwhelmed. A friend of mine, who knew nothing about the challenge I was confronting at that time, called me out of the blue one day and asked if she could come over. She brought a beautiful box of baked goods. Inside was note that said "Just Because. :)"

Those two simple words brought tears to my eyes. They told me "I care about you. You are not alone. I am your friend." The gift also felt like an answer to my prayers from the night before. In short, it was exactly the encouragement that I needed.

If I had not been going through a challenging experience at the time, I wouldn't have appreciated her kindness nearly as much. I would have opened the box, read the note, and said "That's really sweet. Thank you." And then I would have given her a hug. I would have enjoyed those baked goods, but without nearly as much warmth and gratitude. (Gratitude makes cookies taste oh, so much better, by the way!)

Random acts of kindness keep us humble, and it also helps to develop our sense of compassion. I was deeply affected by that gesture, and when the opportunity came time to pass it on, I was ready.

Forgiveness

Forgiveness is the cure to the victimhood mentality. If you want to move on from past hurts, forgive those who have wronged you.

You may be thinking "That's easier said than done!" or perhaps "You don't know what I'm dealing with! You don't understand!" I get it. Sometimes a circumstance, person, or event can hurt you so badly that you think you can't forgive them. Sometimes forgiveness seems too hard, or we don't know how to start, but I will let you in on a secret: it's not for them. It's for you.

When we hold grudges, the person we refuse to forgive is not affected. The person that is burned up and continually hurt with every thought of that person or event is you. It is ok to feel hurt, and I think it's healthy to acknowledge those feelings. It's not ok to let that hurt grow into a grudge. That will only hurt you and the ones that you love.

As I said, bad things happen to good people. I don't know why; that's something you will have to take up with the Almighty. What I DO know is that my trials and hard times have been the catalyst for helping me to grow as a person. Had those events never happened to me, I would not be the person that I am today. Some people are in your life as a lesson.

In his book, "The 4 Doors" Richard Paul Evans constructed a great exercise that I would like to relay to you:

Close your eyes and ask the Lord who you need to forgive. Who comes to mind? If that person is met with an "Oh no! Anyone but them!" response, you have the person you must forgive. I will leave the how up to you. This might involve calling them, talking to them in person, sending an email or snail mail, or simply saying "I forgive you" out loud when you are alone, or in prayer.

Forgiving someone releases the chains of resentment and brings freedom. You should immediately feel the release of tension that you didn't even know you were harboring.

Be Merciful to Yourself

If the person you find impossible to forgive is yourself, you are not alone. We all make mistakes. Some are bigger than others, but we all mess up sometimes, and it's ok. Mistakes are part of being human, part of this wonderful learning experience that we call life.

Often the hardest person for me to forgive is myself. I used to hold myself to an impossibly high standard and beat myself up over every little mistake. That's no way to live. Let it go and forgive yourself. Treat it as a learning experience and move on. Just as there is not a heart on this earth that does not have some sort of scar on it, there is no one currently walking the earth that is perfect either.

I feel that I have made some progress in this area. I think that forgiving oneself is especially challenging for those of us who struggle to transform our perfectionism. I mentioned in Chapter Five that I strived to be the smartest kid in my grade, and what that mindset did to me. I held myself to an impossibly high standard and expected myself to be perfect—on the first try! —at whatever I did.

As you can imagine, this led to a lot of frustration. One memory in particular stands out.

Early in our marriage, when we didn't have much money to spend on non-essentials, we splurged and got a little potter's wheel set. I think it was only about $20, since it was actually intended for kids, but back then we had to think about every purchase we made. I sat down with the wheel, anticipating making the perfect little vase.

Instead, the clay spun around and around in an ugly lump. Turning clay into something recognizable proved harder than the professionals made it look. Because I had no patience, I got a dripping gray blob instead of the little flower vase I had envisioned.

This activity was supposed to be fun! Why did I fail at such a simple task? This toy was worthless! We could have used the money for something else, but instead we wasted it on my stupid idea and ended up with nothing to show for it but an ugly blob of clay!

"I hate this! I'm no good at it!" I plopped the soaking wet hunk of clay back in the bag and stomped away from the table.

My husband laughed. Seriously, I was all mad at myself, and he LAUGHED. "You can't expect to have it come out perfect on the first try, Jen," he said. "You need to be patient with it. Use it to learn."

Then, he had the gall to sit down and work with the potter's wheel to form something halfway decent!

"But you got it on the first try!" I said. "I should have been able to do that."

"No, I had to collapse it back down and restart four times," he said. "You can't be perfect all the time. You need to forgive yourself, and give yourself permission to mess up sometimes. That's how we grow."

After that conversation, I realized that I might have a TINY problem with perfectionism.

Now, I look back at that incident with the clay and think, "If my friend had tried and failed to make that vase, how would I have responded?" I am much tougher on myself than I am on other people. I use this memory as a reminder to tell myself, "It's ok. You're human. You will do better next time."

It's ok to not be perfect. Be merciful. Forgive yourself and move on.

Strategies for Getting Through Challenging Times

Writing

Before I started this chapter, I felt down and out. I was being challenged. Now that I am nearing the end of this chapter, though, I feel much better. Writing is therapeutic. It helps us express our thoughts and feelings, and sometimes it just feels good to get everything out on paper. When I go back and read what I wrote during some of the challenging times in my life, I see that I was in the process of growing into a better person. (Knowing how the story ended also helps me to feel better about it.)

Sometimes it's hard to see how everything will work out in the middle of the story, but it's going to be alright. Every good story has tension, challenges, and resolution. Yours is no different.

Practicing Self-Care

When you are exhausted emotionally, physical self-care is very important. You will deal with your challenges much better if your physical needs are met. That means you need to take that long bath or shower. Make sure that you get enough sleep. Exercise. (I know, I know, but the endorphins will make you feel better when you finish.) Do all the things you know that you should do, but that are too easy to neglect when you feel down.

Affirmations

No, you are not allowed to stop these because the road has gotten a bit rocky! If anything, this is when you need your affirmations the most. You can use the ones you crafted earlier when we talked about limiting beliefs, or you can use others. But just in case you might need a reminder: You are beautiful. You are capable. You are strong. (C'mon now, say them with me!) You can handle whatever life throws at you.

Even if you think you can't do these things, that's why we also talked about praying and drawing closer to God. You don't think you got all this strength on your own, did you? When you think you cannot go on, He will carry you through the hardest parts.

Talk to a Friend

Sometimes, we just need to know that we are not alone. There may not be anything that our friends can do to correct the situation, but it helps to know that someone is here for us—that people are praying for us, and they care. Sometimes it's also a good idea to talk to a friend because they are not as emotionally involved, and they may be able to see things more clearly than you can. It's amazing what a fresh perspective can sometimes do. You might even find after talking to a friend that your problem is not as big as it seems.

Take a Break

You may not be able to swing a week at Disney World, but that does not mean that you can't schedule a break. This one certainly helps me sort through my thoughts and feelings, or even just stop thinking about the challenge at hand for a little while. Taking some time for yourself can be as refreshing as a cool drink of water on a hot day.

Conclusion

We all go through challenges in life. Viewing these challenges as an opportunity for personal growth helps me get through them, and I hope this viewpoint will encourage you as well. It is easy to overlook the bigger picture and miss how the trials you are facing can help you grow. For me, it helps to put everything in perspective. I hope that you find some of these strategies helpful, and that you find the answers you're looking for.

Please remember, it is going to be alright. Change is a constant in our lives. Sometimes it is the only constant. Just because things change, does not always mean that the change will be bad. Things will work out in the end. Your storm will eventually run out of rain.

Chapter 10:
Setting Goals and Chasing Your Dreams

We hear the phrase "Follow Your Dreams!" quite often, but what does it actually mean? Such a lofty concept can be hard to connect with, but it doesn't have to be. Following your dreams can actually be broken down into actionable steps.

First off, you can't follow a dream you don't have. What do you want to do? Where would you like to go, what would you like to see? Are there things you're dying to have, like a new appliance or new decor? Where do you see your life going?

When you are planning a trip, you first have to set a destination. Then you figure out how to get there. The same principle applies to following your dreams. You must set the destination first, or you wind up lost, like driving somewhere unfamiliar without a map. I cannot navigate my way out of a paper bag, for example. There is no telling where I would wind up on my own! However, if I type my destination into Google Maps on my phone and hit "Start," I see all the steps that I need to arrive at my destination.

Following your dreams is much the same. First you decide where you want to go, and then the steps I'm about to describe will lead you to your destination, just like Google Maps. On our journey, you will likely go through some unknown places. Some of those places might be scary when you have to go beyond your comfort zone but if you keep driving, you'll get there!

Where Are You Going?

First things first! Let's set your destination. What do you really enjoy? What are you passionate about? I'm going to walk you through the whole process here, but if you want some very intensive goal setting coaching, I recommend the [Slay Your Goals Planner](). I recently purchased it myself for some of my own goals and I was blown away at how amazingly comprehensive it is.

This first step is one of the hardest parts for me, and it's different for everyone. It's so easy just to set your life on cruise control and let the wind take you where it will, so to speak. But if you want to get somewhere specific, then driving around aimlessly is just a waste of gas. The best way to start is to grab a piece of paper and something to write with. Writing your ideas down makes them more powerful, but we'll get to that in a minute.

Do a total brain dump. I am a bit partial to just jotting everything down in a list, but if you are more visual, you might prefer a mind map or some other method of visual organization. Write down all the things you wanted to be when you grew up. If they're silly, that's ok! We will narrow the list down later. While you're at it, write down all the crazy ideas you had about what to do with your future when you were eighteen or twenty-two, as well. When we are young, we have so many visions of what we want to do with our lives, and the world seems full of possibilities. I think we lose some of that as we get older. You are never too old, however.

Here is an example, if you would like a visual guide:

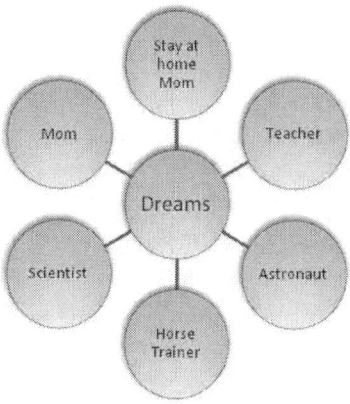

You should have a few items written down, now. Mine might look like this: astronaut, scientist, horse trainer, teacher, mom, stay at home mom.

If you have trouble filling out your list, think about what you played at doing when you were a child. For example, I made tons of little books and stapled them together, so I'm going to add "writer" to my list. You can also think about what you are interested in now, as an adult. For example, do you enjoy gardening, horseback riding, video games, knitting, or woodworking? What about reading, writing, crafts, volunteering, raising backyard chickens, blacksmithing, decorating, photography—or something else entirely? You may not be aware of them at first, and that's ok. Add those ideas to your list, too, when you find them. For example, I just remembered that I also liked being up in front of people in my high school plays, and I like to inspire people, so I'll add a few more words to my list as well.

My expanded list:

- Astronaut
- Scientist
- Horse Trainer
- Teacher
- Mom
- Stay-at-home Mom
- Writer
- Actress
- Movie Star
- Motivational Speaker
- Broadway Performer

Some of my listings, like "movie star" and "Broadway performer" seem unrealistic, don't they? That's ok! This is just a brain dump.

I struggled with finding my passion for a long time. I finally realized that there was a common thread among the things I enjoyed: I loved teaching because I loved inspiring people, and I love being Mom too. When I started Contentment Questing, I had no idea what I wanted to write about, but I found a common thread after a little while. I loved writing the personal development posts the best. In fact, if you look at my blog, you will see that I wrote about many different topics at first, and several months ago narrowed it down to a more specific niche.

So, have you set your destination yet? By doing that, **your dream becomes something new: a GOAL.** Words are powerful because they fuel perspective. Changing the word "dream" to "goal" puts it in a more attainable light. Once again, when you know where you're going, you can make the plan for getting there.

To write this book, I used the same process that I'm about to go through with you. I found my common thread: inspiring and encouraging people. (Guess what I want this book to do for you? Yup! You guessed it!) Committing to the process was a bit scary, because setting a goal and planning how to get there makes it feel more real. That's ok. We grow through new experiences and challenges.

I will use another, simpler, example than writing a book for the process, but this advice will apply to ANY goal that you might want to set. Let's dive in and start the "Google Maps" process of following your dreams!

How to Follow your Dream: The Exact Steps!

Now that our dream has become a goal, we can start mapping the path to our destination. Are you ready? I hope you still have that pencil and paper handy, because we're not done with it yet. Let's start making your dreams a reality!

When setting goals, keep in mind that they must be:

- Attainable
- Measurable
- Actionable
- Have a time frame or deadline

The SMART goal approach is a similar way to set reasonable expectations. "SMART" is an acronym for:

- Specific
- Measurable
- Attainable
- Relevant
- Timely

Lately I've been saying, "I wish we could take the kids to Disney World someday." I need to revise this goal to be more attainable, measurable, and timely. My new statement might look like this:

"I want to save up $4,000 to take the kids to Disney World five years from now."

In this example, the Disney World dream vacation has been turned into a goal: taking the kids to Disney World. Keeping the rules above in mind, let's set an example goal:

I would love to take my kids and my husband to Disney World. I went once as a small child and once as a teen. It was an unforgettable experience. Problem is that it's expensive for a family of four. If I want my dream to happen, I will need to save up money and vacation time. I'm going to have to go through some goal setting.

There is another trick that master goal-slayers use. **Write your goal down on paper and put it where you can see it**. According to the Huffington Post, you are 42% more likely to achieve your goals and dreams if you write them down.

Take that note about your new goal and put it somewhere visible. It can be a post-it note that you put on your planner, or a list that you put on your refrigerator with a magnet. You might put it beside the coffee pot. You can even take a picture of it and set the photo as your lock screen background on your phone. The idea is to write it down and keep it where you will see it every day. Your note will serve as a reminder of what you are working for instead of getting shoved off to the side.

What's your dream? Let's turn it into a goal together!

To Follow Your Dreams, Plan the Work, then Work the Plan

Now that your dream is rewritten as a goal and staring you in the face every day, you are more likely to obtain it. It reminds you of your "WHY."

Now you can subdivide the big goal into smaller goals that are easier to obtain. Every time you hit one of your smaller goals, you get positive feedback! Celebrating when you achieve small goals boosts your morale and helps you to feel like you're making progress towards your goal and your dreams.

Using the example above (going to Disney World), I'll break my overall goal down into smaller ones:

- Open a vacation savings account tomorrow JUST for the Disney Dream Fund.

- $4,000 over five years divides into $800/year to meet our goal. That means we should save about $67/month.

- If there are two paychecks a month, then make it a priority to take $34 out of each paycheck and put it into the Disney Dream Fund.

Now we have some smaller, actionable goals. $34 per paycheck sounds much easier to achieve than the larger task of saving $4000, doesn't it?

Working the Plan

Now comes the hard part, because it requires action. You have to carry through with what you planned out. For example, if I pursue the Disney World goal outlined above, I have to open a savings account tomorrow.

If you are following your dreams, you must make them a priority. Treat that $34 like a bill that you MUST pay. You wouldn't leave a real bill on your desk to pay only if it was convenient. Bills don't work like that. The electric company is not going to be very understanding if you tell them, "I just didn't feel like paying my bill this month. I'll pay next month if I'm in the mood."

Would you like to know a secret about working the plan? The hardest step is the first one. After you have been putting away that $34/paycheck for six months, you probably won't notice it that much. It only takes twenty-one days to form a new habit, and progress begets progress. Take a moment right now and write down your specific goal if you haven't already. You can do this! You might discover that it's not as hard as you imagined once you get going.

Now we have exact, specific, actionable steps to follow your dreams. What smaller steps do you need in order to achieve your dream? Make sure to break them down into actionable chunks with a time frame, like I did above. This process works with any dream, no matter how big or small. If a large dream seems impossible, pick a smaller one to start with. That smaller dream can be related to your big goal, or it could be different entirely. Achieving smaller goals is a great way to build your confidence.

What is Holding You Back?

Now that you have your dream goal written down and broken into specific, actionable steps, with a time frame, let me ask you a question. Is anything holding you back? Maybe you want to become a stay at home mom, but don't have the finances to support it? Perhaps you want to make a certain amount of money per year? Is your dream getting out of the 9-to-5 grind? Does it still seem scary?

Remember: The hardest part of following your dreams is starting.

Common Roadblocks and How to Overcome Them

Fear of Failure

Fear of potential failure when trying to reach your goals holds a lot of people back, and I am no exception. But why? Let me ask you this: **what have you got to lose?** If you don't start saving for a Disney dream vacation, will you ever get it? Probably not. If you want to be a stay-at-home mom, but don't have the finances for it and don't attempt to obtain those finances, will you achieve that goal? Probably not. Dreams must be chased. That means there will be work involved. Sometimes what we want falls right into our lap, but those times are rare.

The work may not be easy, but it will be worth it. Remember your "why." Let's say that you start saving for that Disney vacation, but something breaks and you can't put $68 into savings that month. Let's even say that happens for several months! You still have more in savings now than you did when you started. Your Disney vacation might be delayed, and you might be disappointed, but you still made progress and you can always pick up where you left off. **Persistence wins in the end when you are**

following a dream. Don't be afraid to try again if it does not work out the first time.

You Don't Feel Prepared

Friends, do you remember how you felt when you had your first child, bought your first house, or started your first job? Did you feel prepared? Probably not. (I didn't – Yikes, what have I gotten myself into?!) Your first attempts to act may be imperfect. That's ok! **You can—and should—learn as you go.** Life is full of "on the job training" like that.

I remember looking at my first-born son when he was just a few days old, sleeping peacefully in his cradle. (That "sleeping peacefully" lasted about two minutes, by the way.) I was overwhelmed and exhausted, but I remember thinking about how much I loved him already, and how totally unprepared I was for that phase of my life. Doubts crept in. "I hope I can keep him alive! I can't even keep a plant alive!" I am happy to say that he did survive the infant stage, and toddler stage, and the pre-teen stage is looking pretty good too! I didn't know everything when I started, but I learned as I went, like all of us do.

When following your dreams, remember that starting is the hardest part. It's ok to not know what you are doing at first. We're never too old to stop learning. Your dream is worth following, and you will figure it out!

You're Afraid of What Others Will Think

Yes, I know how silly that sounds. We're all adults, right? But the truth of the matter is that the opinions of those close to us DO matter. I care what my husband thinks and what my friends think. I probably care too much.

Remember the story about accidentally publishing Contentment Questing in Chapter Eight? I decided to take a walk to clear my head, and when I came back, I had a comment from another blogger and four page views. Yikes! The secret was out. I shared it on my Facebook page because I figured I was "all in" at that point, whether I wanted to be or not. I expected either scalding comments or complete disinterest. What I actually got was a lot of support and positive feedback, both from friends and acquaintances!

This book was a "secret project" for three months because I was scared of what others would think. My husband knew and supported me, but I didn't tell anybody else. Finally, when I had about three chapters to go, I decided that confession time had come. I was waiting in the parking lot for my husband to meet me for lunch, and a good friend called me. She told me about some things going on in her life, and on a whim, I finally confessed to her that I was writing a book. I didn't expect her to take it all that seriously. I guess I expected "oh that's nice." And then move on with the conversation. Instead, she responded enthusiastically. She told me how much she enjoyed reading my blog and then offered to introduce me to another friend that she thought might be interested.

Her enthusiastic response gave me confidence (while simultaneously scaring me half to death that this thing might actually WORK). Like when I published my blog, I decided that I was already "all in" so I might as well go for it. I told a few other close friends and family that same week, and they all responded positively.

If you are genuinely concerned about what someone close to you will think if you start taking steps to following your dream, have an honest conversation with them. Sometimes their opinions are not what we think they will be!

Most of all, try to remind yourself that this is your dream and not anyone else's. **Your opinion is more important than all others combined.**

You Feel Inadequate Compared to Others

Let me be perfectly clear on something: **comparing yourself to others is a trap**. Many of us are naturally competitive. I am guilty of comparing myself to others as well, and must remind myself not to make this mistake. There will always be someone better, faster, stronger, more successful. All these comparisons do is encourage frustration and unease.

When you're following your dreams, there is always a learning curve. **Do not allow yourself to be discouraged by someone else's successes**. They are not fighting the same battle that you are. Their circumstances are different, their challenges are different.

Focus on your personal growth instead. Document your progress and hold yourself accountable, but also celebrate the small successes. Using the Disney dream vacation as an example, this process might involve telling your husband, "YES! I have saved $68/month for 6 months, and we have $408 in savings to go towards our Disney dream vacation! Let's go out for ice cream!" Celebrating these small successes and keeping track of them is a powerful tool for motivating yourself to keep moving towards your dream.

Don't worry about what other people are doing. Concentrate on your own journey and your own successes.

The Best Advice for Following Your Dream: Just Start

Yes, that's right: just start. Imperfect action is better than no action. You can learn along the way. A year from now, what will you wish you had started today? Your dreams are important—your GOALS are important.

It's time to plan the plan, then work the plan. Start rewriting your dreams as goals that are attainable, actionable, measurable, and have a time frame. Commit to carrying out your plan. Make it a priority. Remember your "why." Avoid the pitfalls we talked about earlier: fear of failure, fear of what others will think, comparing yourself to others, and lack of preparedness. If getting started scares you, that's ok. Do it anyway!

You can do this. You can achieve anything you set your mind to. I believe in you!

Chapter 11:
Choices

Choices, choices! They may be good, they may be bad, and sometimes they change our lives forever. Life does not provide a "save game" button that we can use to return to our previous state if we mess up. Sometimes we make choices with a lifelong impact when quite young and, not surprisingly, they do not always turn out well. Teenagers are not stereotyped for their wise and well-thought-out decisions! On the other hand, you may look back and be incredibly thankful that you made the choice that you did.

So how do you make good choices? Is there some sort of a blueprint for it? What types of choices most impact our lives?

Some examples of choices that impact our lives are:

- Relationships
- Where to live
- Career
- Level of education
- Who and when/if to marry
- Children – how many, when

Relationships are one of the big choices that are typically made quite young. It seems that the age of "boyfriends" and "girlfriends" is getting younger and younger (or it could just be that I'm getting older!) The choice is not only who to enter into a relationship with but: how involved do you want to get? How satisfied with the relationship are you? What do you want and need from a relationship? All these are things that you will have to answer for yourself, but to get those answers it takes some thought and reflection.

Deciding where to live has obvious life-changing possibilities: different people, different environments, new opportunities to grow as a person. But this choice has consequences: if you move 400 miles away from your parents, they will not be nearby when you need a hug or want a home-cooked meal. The local culture might feel completely different if you move, for example, from the East Coast to the West Coast. We've talked about leaving your comfort zone. This is an example of a big move that could be overwhelming, but also full of potential.

Likewise, your career choices, and the corresponding level of education that you choose to pursue, will have a major impact your life. If you choose to enter the armed forces right after high school, your life will look very different than it would if you chose to pursue a PhD in biology. If you choose to go into landscaping, your work day and your skill set will be different from that of someone who chose to go into business, and therefore spends all their time inside an office building.

Marriage also has huge implications in our lives, and should not be entered into lightly. A good spouse can lift you up and can be the wind beneath your wings. A bad one can tear you down to lower than the lowest low you ever thought possible. (Lower than a snake's belly in a wagon rut, as I've sometimes heard it put.)

Divorce has a huge impact on your emotional and financial life, as well as the lives of others. It puts a huge strain on your finances, because your assets will be split in half. Other worries, such as being concerned about the life-long impact that the divorce will have on your children, are also a factor. Will they feel like they have to choose between their father and mother? Will you get along with an ex-husband for the good of the kids, or will bile rise up in your throat at the sound of his name? Will you be able to tolerate seeing him with another woman? Will you ever be able to love again? Will you ever be able to feel like a whole person again? Where will you live? I would be scrambling to find a job. My life would be turned upside down.

Do you want children? Children are a gift from God, a precious life, and yet choosing to have them is a major decision with life-long implications. You may find yourself gifted with one (or more!) unexpectedly, or you may not receive this gift. You may find your heart longing for them, while you look at other families with sadness and envy. On the flip side, you may choose not to have children. You may be hindered by medical or financial conditions that make having natural children next to impossible. Some people may successfully choose to have 5 children and enjoy the love of a large family. We cannot control everything. Even in situations we cannot control, though, we have a choice in how we react.

These are some pretty heavy things! Thankfully, not every decision we make is life-altering, but thinking about these issues is one of the steps we can use to increase our chances of making good choices

How to Make Good Choices

CorporateWellnessMagazine.com says there are 5 steps to making good choices:

1. Identify Your Goal
2. Gather Information
3. Consider the Consequences
4. Make Your Decision
5. Evaluate Your Decision

Identify Your Goal

Before you make a choice, ask yourself what you're trying to accomplish. Where will this choice take you? You will make better decisions when you think about how they will affect other aspects of your life. Aimlessly making decisions and not thinking about their consequences leads you nowhere.

When I was a senior in high school, I knew that I wanted to go to college. That meant I had to decide where I wanted to go and why. I started by identifying what I wanted: to teach high school science. With that goal in mind, my selection of colleges narrowed. First, the college had to offer teaching degrees. My Dad also put in a condition that I must stay in-state for the first year, which also helped narrow down my choices and made the decision easier!

My goal became: find and in-state college where I could get a science teaching degree.

Gather Information

Another way to ensure that you are happy with your choice is to do your research so you can make an informed decision. For example, when choosing what college I wanted to go to, I started with the major four year universities in my state and collected information about all of them. I visited all of their websites, I looked at brochures, I asked people I knew that had gone there about their experience, and read online reviews. I researched costs per credit hour, housing costs, honors programs, scholarships, and I took into account how far away from home they were. After I had narrowed it down to some favorites, I toured the facilities with my family.

Consider the Consequences

Always consider the consequences of your choice. Please note, however, that there is a difference between considering the consequences and overthinking things to the point that you don't want to make a choice anymore! Try to think about it logically and with as little emotional involvement as possible. Evaluate the consequences that you can reasonably foresee happening.

Praying is also a good way to evaluate your decision. When I am on the fence about something, I'll pray for guidance from my Heavenly Father, who always gives the best advice. The trick is to open yourself up and listen for the answer, which may come in the form of a vague feeling that "this is right." Trust your gut!

This step has saved me from making bad choices many times. The major decisions in your life deserve to be well-thought-out, because you will have to live with those consequences later. In my example earlier, I considered the living conditions in each place that we visited. I considered how well I would fit in with the general atmosphere of the college, and I asked myself: how happy would I be living there?

While a bad choice might have had relatively minor consequences (I might have been a bit uncomfortable for 4 years), another thing I had to consider was how I (or my parents) would pay for it. Would my choice leave me in debt for years to come? Repaying college loans definitely would have a long-term effect on my life.

Make Your Decision

After you identify your goal, gather as much information as you can, and consider the consequences, it is time to take a deep breath and make your decision. This step can be scary, especially when making major, life-changing choices, but at some point, a decision has to be made.

Deciding not to decide is a decision, too. If you choose not to take action, you may let a good opportunity slide by. While it is important to think your decision through, do not delay it for too long, or let fear stop you from doing something that you really want to do. If you have followed the steps above, take the leap and decide.

Evaluate Your Decision

Notice this does not say, "Second guess your decision until you make yourself sick." Evaluating your decision is simply looking back and being able to say, "Yes, I made a good decision and I would make it again," or "No, I gathered as much information as I could and considered the consequences, but if I had known then what I know now, I would have done something else instead."

That's called learning from your mistakes, and it's part of life. You will not make the right decision 100% of the time. If you evaluate your decision and conclude that you made a good one, great! Did you accomplish your original goal? If you did, that's also great! Time to move on to something else.

If you did not make the right decision, or achieve your goal, then ask yourself if your goal is still important to you. If the answer is yes, then go back and start at step one. Figure out how to accomplish your goal this time. Don't beat yourself up over it. Mistakes are valuable learning experiences. You are never too old to fix a mistake, or to move on from one.

Take time to follow this decision-making process for your next major decision. I think that you will find yourself much happier this way, than if you simply rush in with little thought, or procrastinate and let the opportunity slip by.

Chapter 12:

Handling Critics and Criticism

We all have weak points, and criticism is mine. I take everything to heart. Handling critics and criticism is a lesson that I am still learning, but I feel that I have made progress in this department, so I will share what I have learned with you.

Stating Preferences

If I told you that I do not care for water chestnuts (those round, crunchy things found in Chinese food/stir fry), would you think badly of me? Do you think it is an insult to water chestnuts that I don't care for them, but my husband does?

What if I told you that I do not like wearing the color yellow? It's just too bright for my tastes. However, I love seeing it on my sons, especially the youngest, who used to wander away in crowds when he saw something interesting. His bright yellow shirt helped me spot him more easily.

Have I thrown around any insults yet? You are probably thinking "Um... no. So you don't like water chestnuts in Chinese food, or wearing yellow? Those are personal preferences." My husband is not insulted that I don't like water chestnuts—he just makes sure to get some for himself when we go out to eat, because he loves them. My son is not insulted that I don't want to wear yellow while he parades around in a bright yellow Minion t-shirt. Everyone has different preferences.

Likewise, when someone comments with the message "You suck!" they are not stating a fact. They are stating a personal preference.

You will not be everyone's cup of tea. I'm not, and that's ok. Yellow does not stop being bright, cheerful, and easy to spot because I don't care for it on my personal clothing. My son does not stop wearing his yellow shirt just because I do not wear yellow shirts. Water chestnuts still look annoyingly tasty, with a vague resemblance to scallops (which I love), only to disappoint with juicy crunch and odd texture. If someone does not care for you or what you're doing, that doesn't mean you should stop being yourself.

You are unique. You have your own set of amazing gifts, and God gave them to you for a reason. Don't be afraid to let them shine.

How People Treat Others Reflects How They Feel About Themselves

Overall, I feel pretty good about myself, and I try to be kind to people, but not everyone is like that. Some people are unhappy with themselves and with their lives. As a result, they are not always kind. Think of it this way: people say things for many reasons. If someone is going out of their way to be mean, it likely has nothing to do with you at all, and everything to do with them.

Think of a time when you were dealing with a personal challenge, or when you were very tired and run down. Recall how you behaved when you were depleted and in desperate need of self-care. How did you treat the people closest to you, that you love dearly? Were you nice to them, or were you crabby and snappy? Maybe you said something that you did not mean?

When I described my first year of teaching at the beginning of the book, I shared with you how depleted I was. I told you how hopeless I felt, and how my attitude slipped into one of negativity. My attitude in that fifth period class, the tough one, was terrible. I slipped into sarcasm. I yelled. I probably said things to my sweet students that I wish I could take back, because they were not true. I was near the end of my rope, and my nerves were frazzled almost all the time. Let's face it—if an adult is hiding in their room, in a dark corner, and crying during lunch, they are probably barely holding it together in public.

While I struggled very hard to stay professional and did not always succeed, I DID learn a lesson about the harmful effects of sarcasm. When I spoke that way, things went south quickly. My husband loved me enough to tell me, "Stop doing that. It's harmful." But what if I did not have someone in my life that I listened to? Some people are just mad at the world, and they lash out because it makes them feel better temporarily. They may not have anyone to stop them.

When someone is mean to you, it's hard not to take their comments personally. However, it helps me to remember that the people most in need of love are often the ones that act the least loveable. If someone is angry at the world, it's not your fault. They are likely struggling with their own challenges.

Maybe that's why we are told to pray for our enemies. It helps us to forgive, and perhaps they are in a spot where they could really use some prayers.

Why People Can Be Hostile

People are often hostile because they are insecure. Like my sarcasm, lashing out at others is a defense mechanism. It's not a HEALTHY defense mechanism, but we do it in order to keep ourselves "safe." If you constantly push everyone away, you don't risk getting hurt. You also isolate yourself and wind up miserable and lonely, but most people don't think it through that far.

Remember that how people treat you is rooted in how they feel about themselves.

They May Not Mean It Like You Think They Do

Sometimes we take things the wrong way. What we view as an insult might have been intended to have a different meaning.

For example, one Saturday morning during my first year of teaching, I woke up thinking all was normal. It was a peaceful, quiet Saturday in October, and there was a chill in the air. I opened the door to see just how chilly it actually was and froze, blinking at the sea of white in the trees. My sleepy mind tried to process what I saw, and my first thought was "snow." But it was far too warm for that. Then it dawned on me: what I saw was not snow--it was toilet paper! It was so high in the trees I could not get the water from the water hose high enough to shoot all of it down.

I fumed all weekend as we cleaned up. I squirted paper out of the trees while my husband mowed the overgrown yard. He accidentally ran over an extra roll on the ground. Bits of paper exploded from the mower in a white puff and papered our yard all over again. I think at that point I threw up my hands and stomped off.

I heard later that they had put rocks inside the toilet paper rolls and hurled them as high as they could. I'll say this--they had great arms! The "Cu Copper" written on my car windshield was a pretty good indicator of the group that had done it, since that was a punchline to one of my element jokes. In class that week, I had picked a student and had started telling a story about how he was driving along and sped past a cop, saying "See you, Copper!" The joke was intended to help them remember that the chemical symbol for Copper was Cu. They remembered alright.

I hope that you are laughing at this. I am now since I understand what they meant by it. Who knew that driving 30 miles at 2 in the morning to toilet paper a house was a way that teenage boys expressed their affection for their chemistry teacher?

Sometimes we overthink events like this and blow them out of proportion. Sometimes people do not convey exactly what they want to with their gestures. Before we get offended, it might be helpful to remember that.

By the way, please find another way to express your affections to me. Leave me a five star review and a few kind words on Amazon. Just—please don't toilet paper my house at 2am. It creates an awful mess.

Helpful Criticism

Receiving criticism is not fun. Our ego pops on and we go into automatic combat mode, which means that instead of listening, our mind starts thinking about what to say or do to defend ourselves. However, if we can get to the point where we can lay our egos aside, we might actually learn something. Constructive criticism can still hurt a bit, but the difference is, listening to it will help us improve.

There is a company called Bridgewater Associates that embraces a policy that they call "Radical Transparency". They encourage criticism from their employees as a means to help each other improve. They are one of the top companies in their field. You can listen to the full TED Talk on it (though be warned, there is a bit of profanity in it). Ray Dalio, the billionaire CEO, received an email from an employee about a recent meeting. "Ray, you deserve a 'D-minus' for your performance today. You rambled for 50 minutes. It was obvious to all of us that you did not prepare at all. Today was really bad, we can't let this happen again."

Yikes! I can't imagine being a head executive and getting an email like that, but in the culture that he cultivated, that criticism was encouraged as a way to promote learning. He forwarded the email to everyone in the company and asked them to rate his performance. The result was not a good rating, so he reached out to the employee that sent the email and told him that he would do better. This is the response taken from the transcript of the TED talk: *"Listen, I can't trust you to do that. And I (Ray Dalio) say, "Great, I can't trust me to do that, either." And so as a regular protocol, he'll call me up, because he understands that it works well for both of us and works well for the company.*

Whether you would thrive in an environment like that or not, I think this story drives home the point that, if we put our egos aside and try to deal with the problem, criticism can be a means for improvement. My personal opinion is that we need to be nice with our criticism, but from that example above, it is obvious that not everyone agrees with me.

Constructive criticism focuses on how the problem can be resolved without personal insults. Sometimes opening a dialogue with the critic can be beneficial, like it was for Ray Dalio in the above example.

Conclusion

Criticism can be very hard to take gracefully, but at some point, we all have to deal with it. Sometimes it comes from an angry person lashing out at the world because they are unhappy, or from people who have different intentions than what you perceive. What you view as insulting, they may have meant as a joke, or as a way to show that they care. Pray for them and forgive them if you can. Let it roll like water off a duck's back.

When you encounter constructive criticism, you must lay your ego aside, and put yourself in a place that allows you to learn.

Chapter 13:
Building Your Support Network

For a time in college, I tried to go it alone. I interacted with people in class, but I felt largely isolated everywhere else. I ate alone in a cafeteria full of people and watched as everyone else greeted their friends and chatted. This gnawed at me more than anything else, because at home I always sat down with my family for supper. Now, I had no one, and I felt like no one cared. I gobbled my meal and tried not to cry. The smile on my face turned into a mask. Loneliness eats at you, slowly but surely.

Out of desperation, I started to branch out and try to make friends. It was hard, because at that point in my life, I felt extremely shy and insecure. After what felt like many tries, I found a group of friends that I "clicked" with, and college became easier.

That experience taught me that humans do not do well in isolation. We need a support network—people that embrace us, and pick us up when we're down. This network includes our friends, family, and anyone that interacts with and encourages us. These people are our cheerleaders in life.

A Support System Encourages and Instructs You

Attitudes are contagious. That's really good if you hang around positive people, and not so great if your bestie is a Debbie Downer who always sees the worst in everything.

In the first chapter I talked about my own spiral down into a negative attitude. Some of the people that I was around were also pretty negative and tended to complain a lot. While joining them helped me feel a bit better temporarily (since misery loves company), I left the conversation feeling just as bad as I did before it started, and sometimes worse.

I decided to consciously start cultivating the positive attitude that I talked about in chapter two, and I felt much better. Better things started happening to me, and I saw more good things around me. Why? Because I was LOOKING for them.

My sons are a great illustration of this concept. I have one son that can find his shoes 98% of the time. He's always up and ready. He's pretty responsible, and as he gets older, he does more on his own instead of waiting for me to tell him what to do.

But my other son…. he is adorable, sweet, and has lots of good qualities, but 90% of the time he cannot find his shoes to save his life! Why? **Because he doesn't really look for them**. He stands around in one spot, glances around the room, and if he does not see them, declares that he can't find them. Sometimes he even gets so upset that he starts crying because he can't find his shoes. In his mind they are horribly lost, he's going to have to go barefoot forever and the world is probably about to end. Then I walk in, look under his bed, and lo and behold, there are his shoes!

We find what we look for in life. Are you looking for positive things or negative things? Our friends and family also have a bearing on this. My son—the one that can't find his shoes—is getting better at finding them because we have been trying to show him HOW to look for his shoes. Now, instead of standing in the middle of the room and only giving it a glance, he looks under his bed, and in his closet. He no longer gets upset as quickly when he can't find them, because we have started suggesting places for him to look, empowering him with the tools he needs to learn how to find them by himself. We are his support system.

Your support system should be encouraging and build you up. They should also teach you to try something different when what you're already doing does not work well.

Toxic Friends

How do your friends affect your mindset? No one is positive all the time, but we do have general tendencies. When you go home after a chat with your friends, how do you feel? Relieved? Revived and energized? Inspired? Full of hope? Or do you feel hopeless, sad, or angry? Or perhaps just tired with no real reason?

How you feel after visiting your friends can give some insight on whether they are toxic people or a positive influence in your life. In order to succeed, you need to surround yourself with positive people. We may stick with a friend that is toxic at first, because we've known them forever—they're "safe," part of our comfort zone. However, sometimes we need to cut toxic friends out of our lives to grow as people. As the name implies, they poison us and leech off our desires for success. You need to surround yourself with people that will feed and nurture those dreams, not suck them dry.

Sometimes it is not possible to cut toxic people from our lives completely, and I personally have a very hard time giving up on my friends. However, if someone is acting toxic, I can limit the amount of time I spend with them. Friends have an enormous influence over our lives. That's why it's so important that we choose wisely.

Sometimes people give up and focus just on surviving, going through the motions of everyday life. To me, that is one of the saddest things that can happen, but they have to decide for themselves to make a different choice.

You can't force anyone to change. **The only person that you can change is yourself.**

How to Find Your Support Network

Some people refer to your support network as your "tribe." Some are fortunate enough to be born into great families that love and support one another unconditionally. Other families do not function that way. So how do you find your support network?

We obviously can't change the family that we were born into, but you can and should choose your friends wisely. We start making friends at a very young age, either in daycare or when we start school, and while I don't keep in touch with any of my friends from kindergarten, I do keep in touch with some from high school. I love these ladies! Experience only made our friendships stronger.

Once you get out of school, friends can be a little harder to find. When I first started staying home with my oldest son, I felt incredibly lonely. My friends were all busy. My car blowing a head gasket shortly before I gave birth didn't help, either. I really was trapped at the house, relying on my Mom to take me to the grocery store, or anywhere else I needed to go during the day. Even after we managed to gather enough money to get a second car, I still felt an aching need for new Mommy friends.

One day at the park, I saw this very pretty lady with adorable twins. My own son was about 9 months old at the time. I said hello to her and we got to talking. Our boys are

11 now; we're still great friends, and so are the boys! She is as beautiful on the inside as she is on the outside.

Have the courage to walk up and say hi to people. It can be a bit intimidating to strike up a conversation with a complete stranger, but it's a great, no-obligation way to meet people. Going to church can also be a great way to meet people, and so are mommy groups, interest groups and trips to the library. Just about anywhere can be a place to make friends. The trick is to make the first move yourself. If you are an introvert or are very shy, you may be thinking, "No way!" But there is a non-creepy and non-awkward way to introduce yourself to someone in an informal setting:

Choose someone that you think looks nice or interesting. Notice what they're doing, or think of something situation-related to open the conversation. When I met my friend at the park, I said "Oh my goodness, your twins are adorable!" Once you start talking, find something you have in common, or ask a question. In my example, I asked "How old are they?" And then I responded with my own son's age when she answered. You can keep up this back-and-forth for some time to gather information. People love to talk about themselves, and one of the most flattering things you can do for someone is express interest in them, while gradually revealing a bit about yourself.

The good thing about this method is, if you discover that this person is not as interesting as you thought, you can always say, "It was really nice meeting you! I hope you have a great day!" and walk away.

To offer another example of this process: I was at a state park recently, and was washing my hands in the bathroom. Another lady was at the other sink, and I looked around for the soap. She was actually the first one to speak to me, and said, "Oh, the soap is right over here, just squeeze in and get some." (She was in a wheelchair, so there was only so much she could maneuver out of the way.)

I responded "Thanks! I'm kind of surprised that they actually had soap here. A lot of the state parks are always out."

Because I had found common ground in the fact that we were both at a state park, we continued the conversation. A smile lit up her face and she said, "I know!" Then, she offered a bit more information with "We just love the state parks here, though."

At this point, I could have continued the conversation several ways, but I tried to hurry because I knew my husband and kids were outside waiting on me. If I had wanted to continue the conversation further, I could have asked her "Do you come here often?" or "Where are you from?" or possibly "What's your favorite thing to do here? What can you recommend?"

When we came out of the bathroom, both of our husbands were outside waiting on us, wearing expressions that said, "You made a friend in the bathroom?! You were taking forever talking while we were out her waiting on you!" As I left to go with my husband and she with hers, she called out, "I hope you guys have a great time here!"

I responded with "Thanks! You too!"

As you have read the method twice now, I want you to notice something: in neither instance did I get their name or a way to contact them at first. Wait until you have had a good conversation, and then, if the person interests you enough, ask their name. Usually, "Oh, by the way, I'm (your name)" works pretty well. If I want to keep in contact with them, I usually ask if we can connect on social media. That way I have a way to contact them again, but without risking too much personal information like my phone number.

Do Your Friends Believe in You?

I must say, I have some really great friends. When I finally got up the courage to tell them that I was writing a book, which is something that is a bit out of my comfort zone, they were excited and incredibly supportive. They took me seriously. They believed in me. Their support was a bit daunting at first, to be honest. It gave me hope that this would get off the ground, but with that hope came fear.

After I told them, I went to have lunch with my husband, and I was so fidgety that I could hardly concentrate on my meal. Do you ever feel like that when you try something outside of your comfort zone? He told me "You are afraid because you now have hope. Often times fear will overpower that hope, but don't let it." I looked into his eyes and I knew that he was right.

I told my husband that I was balking because of the risk involved in publishing this book. Getting a book professionally edited and published requires some investment. My husband reminded me that his pilot license was an investment as well, but I had told him dreams were worth following. He looked deep into my eyes and said "Your dreams are worth following too."

When I told one of my friends about it, she was ecstatically enthusiastic, and when I asked her if she would be willing to help me out with it, she said "Well, OF COURSE!" She also offered to introduce me to another friend that she thought might help. Her enthusiasm and faith floored me. (And scared me half to death, because I knew I was near the point of no return).

If my friends had blown the idea off, or discouraged me instead of offering so much encouragement, this book would be nothing more than an incomplete Word document on my laptop. If my husband had said "I don't know…" to investing in the publishing of this book, I would have stopped before I was finished.

Your friends, your family and the other people in your support network should believe in you and encourage you when you're down. They should give you the courage to push past your insecurities and out of your comfort zone. There is not one person strong enough to make it entirely on their own. We need our family, our friends, and other people that love us unconditionally to keep investing in us, and help us invest in ourselves.

Chapter 14:

Wrapping It All Up

I have been referring to you as my "friend" throughout this book, and that's what you are. But you are also more: you are a Pearl. Pearls start as a bit of grit that gets into an oyster. The oyster takes that grit and builds a hard shell around it. Just like that pearl, our lives are full of adversity and challenges that we must overcome. The more we try to overcome those challenges, and the more we grow as people, the more beautiful we become.

Now the bad news: it takes work. You see, my Pearl, no one has the power to change your life for you. That is a decision that only you can make. I have outlined how to approach those changes and given you the tools to act on it. The rest is up to you. Your dreams are possible if you set goals and work to achieve them. Your choices will define your life and determine your course. Think them through and make them count.

When you **decide** to change your life is when it will change – when you take action. In addition to setting goals and making good choices, there are some other behaviors that you will need to let go of, like worrying. Worry is like a parasite that sucks away our joy. Don't let it get your happiness. Cast it off and don't pick it back up again. Instead, replace worry with its more productive sibling, concern and practice mindfulness to center yourself when you start to feel stressed out. Determine what you need to take care of yourself when you are in a position of taking care of others, because this involves giving of yourself.

When you take time to restore your own resources, your gifts to others are more effective.

Practice gratitude. When we start remembering the blessings that we already have, it shifts our mindset. You see, my Pearl, we find what we look for. If you are looking for the blessings and the good things in your life, you will find them. It paints a stark contrast to looking at what you don't have, which only brings discontent. Comparing yourself to others is also a trap that breeds discontent. Remember that you are unique. There is no one else in the world quite like you. Often, we do not see the challenges that other people face. Likewise, you have your own unique challenges to overcome. When you are trying to make a change, don't compare yourself to others. Look at how far you have come in your own journey.

You may have to work past some negative emotions that stem from past hurts. My Pearl, there is not a heart on this planet that does not have some scars on it. Don't play victim. Take responsibility for your life and where you are now. Forgive those who have wronged you—not for them, but for yourself. While you are at it, you should also forgive yourself. Stop beating up on yourself for past mistakes. Learn from them and move on.

I wish that I could tell you that your life will be smooth sailing from here on out if you do all these things, but that's not true. You will still be faced with hard times. In truth, we need those hard times because they are a chance to grow. If you are comfortable all the time, you will not be motivated to make changes. Some of the best things that happen are the result of a hard time we went through, or a challenge that we faced, which we used as a spring board for growth.

People are not going to be nice all the time. How I wish that I could change this for you, because more than any other area, I struggle with this one the most. It helps me to remember that people who are hurting will hurt other people. Try to let it roll like water off a duck's back and move on. Some types of criticism may sting a bit, but still be helpful. Use it to fix what you can, and don't take it too personally. Remember that you are a pearl. Not everyone will be able to see your shine, but if that is the case, then it's their loss. You do not necessarily need to change just because someone disapproves of you, or something you do. They may be very unhappy with their lives, and their insults may simply be a result of their own unhappiness.

Turn to the friends and family who believe in you for support. These people are your cheerleading squad. They love you and support you, and hopefully they also love you enough to stop you if you're about to make a terrible mistake. Trust them, treasure them. If you do not have a strong support network, start building one. Limit your time around toxic people and look for ones that will build you up. Pay attention to how you feel after you hang out with them. No one can go it alone—we all need the love and support of our friends. They encourage us when we are weary, pick us up when we are down, and believe in us and our dreams.

My Pearl, I have tried to give you all the tools that I know of to change your life. When you decide to change your life is when it *will* change – when you take action to start. You are your own rescue, as Lisa Nichols is fond of saying. In order to do that, you have to take action! All the books in the world will not help you if all you do is read them.

My Pearl, you are so amazing, and you don't even realize it. Most people don't. I want a better life for you. I want you to be happy. I want you to feel unstuck. You are beautiful, whether you realize it or not. If you don't feel like a pearl yet, it may be because you are still inside the oyster. No one can see how beautiful you are in there! You have to come out! When you do, I can't wait to see you shine! ♥

About The Author:

Hi! I'm Jennifer! I'm so glad that you picked up a copy of this book. It's my goal to give you the actionable steps that you need to take in order to improve your life. Life is too short to spend simply going through the motions and not enjoying. I blog at contentmentquesting.com where I share inspirational articles with actionable, relevant advice for finding joy in all the little things in your life.

I would describe myself as pretty ordinary. I am married to the love of my life, Shanon, to whom this book is dedicated. We have two sweet sons that light up our world. We live in a small community in Arkansas. I was a teacher for 3 years at a small school district where I taught 7 different science subjects in 3 years, but more importantly than science, I taught students. The people in our lives are some of the greatest treasures.

One of the secrets to living life to the fullest is to love unconditionally. I try to live it as well as write about it. This book comes from the heart and is from me to you. I believe in you. You are special, unique, and valuable. There is no one else in this world quite like you.

I would love to hear from you. Please visit me on the blog at contentmentquesting.com or send me an email at Jennifer@contentmentquesting.com.

Made in the USA
Columbia, SC
26 January 2021